THE WHOLE STORY

The Wedding of Science and Religion

NORMAN CARROLL

www.spiritualsummit.net

PACEM IN TERRIS PRESS

*Devoted to the global vision of Saint John XXIII,
prophetic founder of Postmodern Catholic Social Teaching,
and in support of the search for a Postmodern Ecological Civilization,
which will seek to learn from the rich spiritual wisdom-traditions
of Christianity and of our entire global human family.*

www.paceminterrispress.com

Copyright © 2018 Norman Carroll
All Rights Reserved

ISBN-13: 978-0999608869
ISBN-10: 099960886X

*My personal thanks to Mary Moran who typed this manuscript.
With gratitude to Keith Coponi for all the drawings in this book.
Quotations from books by Ilia Delia with permission from Orbis Books.
Cover photo from Shutterstock.*

*Pacem in Terris Press publishes scholarly books directly or indirectly related to
Catholic Social Teaching and its commitment to justice, peace, ecology,
and spirituality, and on behalf of the search for a Postmodern Ecological Civilization.*

*In addition, in order to support ecumenical and interfaith dialogue, as well as dialogue
with other spiritual seekers, Pacem in Terris Press publishes scholarly books from other
Christian perspectives, from other religious perspectives, and from perspectives
of other spiritual seekers that promote justice, peace, ecology,
and spirituality for our global human family.*

*Opinions or claims expressed in publications from Pacem in Terris Press
represent the opinions and claims of the authors and do not necessarily represent
the official position of Pacem in Terris Press, the Pacem in Terris Ecological Initiative,
Pax Romana / Catholic Movement for Intellectual & Cultural Affairs - USA
or its officers, directors, members, and staff.*

PACEM IN TERRIS PRESS
is the publishing service of

PAX ROMANA
Catholic Movement for Intellectual & Cultural Affairs
USA
*1025 Connecticut Avenue NW, Suite 1000,
Washington DC 20036
www.paceminterris.net*

ABOUT THE AUTHOR

An extraordinary life! Norman Carroll, following graduation from secondary school, studied seven years for the Roman Catholic priesthood in the seminary of the Franciscan Friars at Graymoor, New York. Then, he studied four additional years, to become a Doctor of Chiropractic which he practiced for thirty-one years while serving in 1971 as president of the Florida Chiropractic Association. During this time, he pursued his abiding passion for spirituality and theology by ordination to the diaconate in 1979. Finally, he gained his Doctor of Ministry in 1994 from the Graduate Theological Foundation.

Dr. Carroll initiated in 1996 a fifteen-year career of preaching over two hundred parish retreats throughout the United States. His missions included hundreds of power-point slides on the subjects of Understanding Biblical Wisdom,

Behold the Man, and the Second Vatican Council. Dr. Carroll published in 2010 his first book *Miracles, Messages, and Metaphors: Unlocking the Wisdom of the Bible*. Richard Rohr, OFM wrote accordingly, "If spiritual leaders like Norman Carroll do not share their biblical wisdom, I fear Christianity will become insular and self-serving." and William Byron, SJ, "As friend of Raymond Brown and Joseph Fitzmyer [eminent scripture scholars], it pleases me immensely to see their scholarly work translated into useful and understandable terms."

Deacon Carroll also chairs the At Risk Children Foundation which houses, feeds, and educates orphans in Haiti. (For more information, consult: *https://www.savethekids.com*)

Deacon Carroll has during the last five years devoted himself to authoring his latest book, *The Whole Story: The Wedding of Science and Religion*. It captures the ultimate goal of science and religion bonding together to explain the magnificent relationship of creator and created in creation. Truly, the hostility between science and religion could be terminating. Pursuant to this book's content, they might be starting an eternal love-affair of complementary covenant.

ABOUT THE BOOK

THE WHOLE STORY: THE WEDDING OF SCIENCE AND RELIGION is more than a book: actually, it's a revolutionary call to personal, societal, and cosmic wholeness. Today, we suffer from disastrous divisions within the four fundamentals of culture: politics, education, economics, and most importantly, religion. Christianity still states as fundamental to its traditional set of teachings, "God has created Eden and its two residents, Adam and Eve, from nothing." Science responds, "Such ideas represent an example of illogical, unscientific, and juvenile thinking."

Science and religion have been waging this battle for many centuries, and all humanity is losing. The reason? Science views religion as insisting on outdated modes of expressing its truths, and thereby refusing to participate in the continuing progression of human thought and belief. Meanwhile, religious believers deem science as profane and godless. The struggle promotes tribal suspicion and discord throughout all human culture, and prevents full participation in worthy endeavor.

This book "tackles", and answers this all-important conflict including even the long-debated and difficult problem of evil, and does so in understandable language even for non-professionals. The singular extraordinary importance of this resolution is unmistakable.

To solve this bitter fundamental hostility, the scientific community must be willing to seek truth with an open mind wherever it leads, even into the halls of religion. Contrarily, believers must accept God's presence not as a separate quasi-human being (a sky-god) but as a relationship of love present in all creation.

Then, science and religion together can lead humanity to a new world order that would prioritize truth and compassion. Imagine our living transforming into a magnificent search and discovery of love in our no-longer ordinary daily lives. Indeed, we could come to experience the words of Gary Zukav: "Love heals everything, and love is all there is."

TABLE OF CONTENTS

Introduction	1
1. Parts & Wholes	16
2. Our God of Wholeness	31
3. Life in the Trinity	48
4. Abounding Love	61
5. Continuing Creation	79
6. Universal Evolution	94
7. Christ of the Cosmos	111
8. Church in Crisis	124
9. Destined beyond Time & Space	142
10. That They All May Be One	155
Other Books from Pax Romana Press	172

INTRODUCTION

I don't see any conflict between science and religion. Religion has to accept the science of the day and penetrate it to the mystery. The conflict is between the science of 2000 BCE and the science of 2000 CE. And that is what we have in the Bible."

JOSEPH CAMPBELL

With thinning white hair, stooped shoulders, and face etched with deep lines, he cries out: "Danger!" "Crisis!" "Emergency!" But the younger, with sharp intellect, bright eyes, and crisp tone, counters: "Connections!" "Opportunity!" "Freedom!"

These two are witnessing with us today's religious-cultural breakup, but all peer through different lenses. Could such cries represent the core of the hostility pervading our culture: including politics, education, economics, and the heart of culture: religion? Is it possible we must learn to view all reality including each other in a way we have never perceived before?

Fritjof Capra, celebrated physicist, exclaims, "We find ourselves in a state of profound worldwide crisis. It is a complex multidimensional crisis whose facets touch every aspect of our lives. It is a crisis of educational, moral, and spiritual dimension: a crisis of a scale and urgency unprecedented in human history."[1] Capra is not exagger-

---

[1] Fritjof Capra, The Turning Point, Science Society and the Rising Culture (NY: Bantam Books, 1988), 21.

ing, but his words, and those of other insightful thinkers, are not "sinking in."

For most of us, "It's business as usual." For example, wealthy outrageous entertainers and entrepreneurial politicians such as Rush Limbaugh and Donald Trump still deny humanity's role in the agonizing ecological cry from mother Earth. What's worse; such opportunists are revered by millions. Deaths from crazed mass murderers rise, and we provide them greater access to weapons. Our national education achievement levels decline while global information and communication soar.

Despite its desperate need, religion is becoming truly irrelevant while women, gays, and most minorities are successfully flexing their cultural muscles. Others cling desperately to traditional values and struggle fiercely against this cultural revolution. It's a new world! It's the second axial age!

Karl Jaspers, the twentieth-century German philosopher, wrote of the first axial age (400 – 800 BCE): "The spiritual foundations of humanity were laid simultaneously and independently in China, India, Persia, Judea, and Greece. And these are the foundations upon which humanity still exists today."[2] This marked, according to Joseph Campbell, "The awakening of man's reason. No longer is he informed and governed by the animal powers. No longer is he guided by the analogy of the planted Earth, no longer by the courses of the planets but by reason."[3]

We can easily understand the huge impact of this first axial age as mankind began depending, not on objects in reality that were beyond control, but on the greater use of intellect, and humanity's be-

---

[2] Karl Jaspers, *The Way to Wisdom: An Introduction to Philosophy* (New Haven, CT: Yale University Press, 1951), 98.

[3] Joseph Campbell, *The Power of Myth* (NY: Doubleday 1988), 28.

coming conscious of it. Women and men were beginning to understand themselves in the mirror of their own life experience, and fancy themselves as central and primary on Earth.

However, today's second axial age, beginning in the mid-20th century, is exploding with even more shattering radical change. Raimon Panikkar, philosopher and author, writes in 2010:

> *The world itself has changed. Much has happened in this century; much that is new: two world wars and over a hundred major armed conflicts since 1945 have ravaged the Earth; colonial empires have disappeared; technocracy has spread over the entire planet; religious traditions have mingled; whole peoples have been uprooted; mentalities have changed.*[4]

Reality is transforming profoundly, and we are changing with it. Enormous stores of information are now accessible, but wisdom is lacking. It's no wonder that, with the sands of certainty shifting beneath our feet, we are losing our societal balance. Young and old, black and white, male and female, East and West, progressive and conservative: all distrust one another.

War and violence are "front and center;" political compromise is giving way to the terrors of vicious ideology threatening the very usefulness of democracy, as we once knew it. Finally, and foundationally, religion and science are engaging in bitter struggle. In a word, many of us neither know nor trust God nor each other: we seem to have lost our way.

The theologian, Ewert Cousins, writes,

> *This second axial period is communal, global, ecological, and cosmic. It is not merely a shift from first axial period conscious-*

---

[4] Raimon Panikkar, *The Rhythm of Being the Unbroken Trinity* (Maryknoll, NY, Orbis Books, 2010), xxv.

ness; it is an advance in the whole evolutionary process, challenging world religions to bring about a new integration of sacred and secular energies into total global human energy.[5]

We have heretofore depended on religion (Christianity in the West) for our wisdom-stories of cultural survival, but now, even religion, as a fundamental component of culture, bleeds with deep severe wounds; but strangely, its hurt is largely self-inflicted.

Even Pope Francis questioned his own administration in December 2014: "I wonder about ourselves, what is within the church that makes the faithful unhappy?" Several days later, he answered his own question: "It's the sickness of those who insatiably try to multiply their powers ... victims of careerism and opportunism ... fruit of hypocrisy that is typical of mediocre and progressive spiritual emptiness."

---

[5] Ewert Cousins, *Christ of the 21st Century* (Rockport, MA: Element, 1992), 710.

Rabbi Abraham Heschel exclaims insightfully,

> *It is customary to blame secular and anti-religious philosophy for the eclipse of religion in modern society. It would be more honest to blame religion for its own defeats. Religion declined not because it was refuted, but because it became irrelevant, dull, oppressive, and insipid.*[6]

Heschel adds, "Religion is expected to answer man's ultimate questions."[7]

Unfortunately, today, religion in general and Christianity in particular, are providing few answers to these ultimate questions, such as: why value each other's dignity? How can a God of love allow such egregious evil? Does the health of mother Earth carry priority? Why do we capitalists prioritize profit over justice, even as the southern hemisphere and others starve to death? Is my belief system truly superior to yours? Can an exploding Cosmos destroy our traditional God? Does violence offer a legitimate option in addressing needed fundamental change?

Sadly, religion remains "stuck" on questions of <u>doctrine</u>; for example, original sin perpetrated on all humanity by the mythic Adam and Eve; <u>ritual</u>; for example, exact words repeated week after week, year after year in the same manner and exact spot, and <u>control</u>; for example, birth control is affirmed sinful when 90% of the faithful women of childbearing age practice such with impunity. Our world stands in dire crisis, and religion (like Nero) continues to fiddle, still in its anachronistic mode.

---

[6] Abraham Heschel, *God in Search of Man: A Philosophy of Judaism* (New York: Farrar, Strauss, and Giroux, 1976) 3.

[7] Heschel, God in Search of Man, 3.

The divisive hostility and distrust of science and religion stands, however, as the root cause of our emergency, for the crisis results from our cataclysmic lack of knowledge of God, his/her design of the universe, and all that flows from it. One could object that such divine mystery is not for us to understand anyway. However, skilled theologians and scientists have been exploring for several generations "the divine milieu" with amazing salutary insights and explanations.

We, in these pages, will accomplish the impossible. We will contradict the overwhelming opinion that science and religion represent bitter enemies. Rather, we will discover and probe their complementary embrace, and the actual need one has for the other: in a word, their wedding, and <u>you</u> are invited.

Within its tradition, dogmatic religion has its place. However, a burgeoning Cosmos of unimaginable scope with its Big Bang mother lode, humanity's catastrophic difficulties, and Earth's menacing challenges cry for theological and cultural exploration and solution.

Declarations of doctrine, even if true, do not "fill the bill." Cardinal Ratzinger, later Pope Benedict XVI, gave witness over forty years ago, "A great gulf is developing between the world of faith and science, a gulf that seems unbridgeable so that faith is very largely impracticable."[8]

Despite the tragic official silence of church and laboratory, an aforementioned cadre of scholars has been plumbing the depths of these murky scientific and religious waters. Their efforts are fundamental to understanding our current religious-scientific cultural chaos. Names such as Thomas Berry, David Bohm, Judy Cannato, Teilhard de Chardin, Ilia Delio, John Haught, Diarmuid O'Murchu, Raimon Panikkar, and Brian Swimme among others, come to mind.

Sadly, most Christians don't even recognize their names, much less their work. Further, their profound insights have proven heady for most non-professionals. However, the contributions of these scholars and others remain too prophetic and salvific to be buried in tomes on dusty bookshelves. Therefore, these desperately needed pages will unwrap a new exciting cosmological-theological story in a *readable way for all thoughtful people to understand*. This book reveals our opportunity to comprehend a new cosmology, appreciate healthy religion, integrate both, and heal the crises of our day.

You can proceed without fear of sacrificing your own religious tradition; indeed, that worthy tradition will be updated and deepened. Most importantly, you will journey down a road of unforgettable search that will transform your worldview, your priority of values, and, yes, even your lifestyle. We have mentioned the marvelous pioneering work of many scholars. We must particularly note here our indebtedness to the work of Ilia Delio whom we will quote extensively in these pages. Of reality, Thomas Berry exclaims:

---

[8] Joseph Ratzinger, *Faith and the Future* (Chicago, Franciscan Herald Press, 1971), 15.

It's all a question of story. We are in trouble just now because we do not have a good story. We are in-between stories. The old story – the Genesis account of how the world came to be, and how we fit into it – is not functioning properly, and we have not learned the new story.[9]

These pages tell the new story in a readily understandable way. Diarmuid O'Murchu quotes Bede Griffiths:

We are in a stage of transition between the breakup of the ancient cultures and the birth of a new civilization ... a new structure has to be found and this will necessarily be universal, as we now belong irrevocably to one world.[10]

This book introduces and identifies this story with its new structure. It blends the fundamental elements of the Judaic-Christian tradition and others with the findings of science, and invites you to their surprising and magnificent love affair. This extraordinary topic divides into ten chapters, but they are all interdependent like the central ingredients of a marvelous casserole. I urge you to savor the whole literary dish, for it will vigorously fortify your search for the meaning of our current lives, where we are journeying, and how to arrive.

We begin in Chapter 1 by viewing the new insight that scientists call holism. You the reader, and I the author, recognize each other as whole individual persons, but we are also parts of humanity, a greater whole. Humanity, the whole, is also part of the whole planet which is also a part of our whole galaxy, which is also a part of

---

[9] Thomas Berry, "The New Story," *Teilhard in the 21st Century. The Emerging Spirit of Earth*, Editors, Arthur Fable & Donald St. John, (Maryknoll, NY. Orbis Books, 2003), 77.

[10] Diarmuid O'Murchu, *Evolutionary Faith* (Maryknoll, N.Y. Orbis Books, 2002), 197.

the whole Cosmos. Every being is a whole and part of a whole simultaneously: we call these beings, holons.

This holonic framework applies most importantly to us humans in our spiritual world. We are designed to participate in an astounding wholeness: God and all created beings united in one ultimate whole of loveliness. Our realizing that we belong literally to each other in the same whole family will begin turning our competitive behavior into cooperative, war into peace, and self-seeking into lovemaking.

Even more outstanding, we understand in Chapter 2, the spiritual dimension of these surpassing relationships as applying to us and to God. God is not a bearded being in heaven: not bearded, not a being, and not in some heaven. God is foundational to all created beings that are also interrelated with each other. Forget the traditional notion of an objective separate God either pulling the strings of creatures, or failing to do so like a Geppetto controlling Pinocchios.

God will not tolerate separated, interrupted, or incomplete love. God lives and loves uniquely and fully in every created being. These pages call on you to expand your vision to include this ultimately foundational God of the whole universe in all its bountiful beauty. Experience the unimaginable!

Chapter 3 reminds us that we, as Christians, know God as Trinity. However, we tend to think of Trinity as an unintelligible theological reference to the life of God totally removed from our living. Indeed, Christianity has struggled for centuries to describe Trinity even with the childlike metaphor of a shamrock with its three leaves.

Rather, our Triune God resides in each of us and in our communities and experiences, as mutually creating, saving, and energizing relationships of love. Again, this truth surely helps to heal our geopolitical power-plays, our economic systems that feed on greed, our worship of the military complex, and our personal hostilities.

We Christians profess *God as love,* 1 John 4:16. God actually surpasses love, but love represents our best description. All true love, including human love, is of God. The more universal, unwavering, and deep our love, the more godly we become. Loving, as witnessed in Chapter 4, defines divinity, and the summit of human behavior. My dear friend, the more we love, the more we are of God. Do you, do I, see ourselves and our religious institutions today as expressions of love?

Most Christians believe God is an objective person who created Adam, Eve, and all reality from nothing. But wait! Scientists claim the "Big Bang" is the origin of the Cosmos 13.7 billion years ago. So, the "sixty-four-dollar questions": which came first: God or the "Big Bang", or is there another explanation? Furthermore, if God created, why? Did God create from nothing?

Remember, Genesis does not state God created from nothing. (See Gen. 1:1.) Additionally, why did God stop creating, or did he/she? Do we participate in creating? These questions and others beg for resolution, and we will address them and many more in an enlightening Chapter 5 entitled, Continuing Creation.

Do you, whether Christian or not, accept evolution? Despite the obvious evidence of our physical, intellectual, spiritual progression, and even evolution of new species (for example, the human species), many Christians deny incredibly this evolving process: thus, today's disconnect between science and religion which, we dismantle in Chapter 6.

Many religious zealots claim evolution is mere theory which seeks to eliminate the possibility of a creating God. Stephen Jay Gould, famed paleontologist and biologist, writes:

> *In the American vernacular, 'theory' often means imperfect **fact** – part of a hierarchy of confidence running downhill from fact to theory to hypothesis to guess ... thus, creationists argue: evolution **is only a theory.***[11]

Actually, the **scientific** use of the word "theory" to describe evolution may be likened to the "theory" of two plus two equals four. In popular parlance, this is hardly raw theory, but accepted fact. It's time that we Christians acknowledge evolution as fact at least as firmly as two plus two equals four, and accept that healthy religion has nothing to fear from any truth.

Darwin emphasized the difference between his two great and separate accomplishments: establishing the fact of evolution and natural selection, to explain reality's continuing onward march. If we, whether Christian or not, accept obvious evidence, we must accept evolution. Let us state with clear certainty: Christianity and science are truly wedded because they both represent truth, and mutually seek truth from their own perspective. We explore in Chapter 6 their intimate relationship that calls us to embrace spiritual underpinnings while appreciating scientific vision.

Where is Jesus Christ in all this talk of evolution? Most importantly, let's remember that the name "Jesus" refers to the historical person from Nazareth; whereas, Christ is God's continuing saving and risen presence in Jesus and all creation, past, present and future. Christ is beyond the historical Jesus, and seeks birth continuing throughout the whole Cosmos.

Paul writes, "*We are well aware that the whole creation, until this time, has been groaning in labor pains.*" (Rom. 8:22) This is incarnation in its full sense (*pleroma*). Jesus becomes the model for the whole birthing

---

[11] Stephen Jay Gould, "Evolution as Fact and Theory," *Hen's Teeth and Horse's Toes* (New York: W.W Norton, 1994) 254-262.

of Christ in us and in our corner of this evolving Cosmos. Chapter 7, therefore, explores in depth this personal and communal birthing throughout creation, in my life and yours.

Chapter 8 probes the role of church in this expansive vision of the entire creation in God and evolving toward God. An outstanding problem exists however: some churches still resist embracing the powerful changes of the second axial age. They shout: "Support the war!" "Women belong in the kitchen!" "We are the true church!" "Gays can't marry!" Etc. They bespeak an "old time religion", a cultural age long gone.

Any church clinging to such anachronistic views becomes irrelevant, and, when its views oppose those of Jesus, its founder, that church has lost its moorings. By contrast, the church that empowers all people evolving in Christ and wholeness, fulfills its mission in the 21st century. Such a church fosters that mystical union for which Jesus pleaded, and gave his life.

The year was 1969; the singer, Peggy Lee; her hit song: *Is That All There Is?* The lyrics tell the story of several happy human events (including life itself). They end, however, in deep disappointment as the chorus repeats: *"Is That All There Is?"* We find the solution to humanity's and Peggy Lee's doleful question with that most joyous answer: ongoing evolution through death and resurrection.

Chapter 9 pictures our evolving journey from the Trinitarian God of love before the Big Bang to God's presence in us now and beyond time and space. Seeking ever greater truth and love comprises the energy and the attraction of progression in Earthly life. As each moment of our ever-evolving life springs forth, the Risen Christ presides in us and through us in a new and dynamic way, and liberates us from the boredom and depression from which so many suffer.

In Chapter 10, we recall that Jesus prays, "*May they all be one; just as Father, you are in me and I am in you ...*" (John 17:21) In this prayer, Jesus is not referring to Christian denominations coming together, for there was no Christianity in his time. Rather, Jesus cries out for his disciples to seek oneness with God through and in him and God's beloved creation. However, all his disciples are not limited to those physically present to him nor exclusively to believers, for we know God's beloved includes all creatures in the entire exploding Cosmos.

All this suggests an amazing vision of the unity of God and the whole creation in a Spirit-filled union of universal eternal love. What a privilege to seek with you the boundless horizons of Paul's words: "No eye has seen and no ear has heard what the mind of man cannot visualize; all that God has prepared for those who love him." (1 Cor. 2:9.)

This book will thus introduce you to this ever-expanding vision of a munificent God, Cosmos, and us Earthen travelers. It will challenge you to shed the shackles of theological and scientific hostility for an amazing panoramic epiphany: God, Cosmos, and humanity bonded together always giving birth to new expressions of divinity while evolving moment to moment in one Christic whole.

"Medievalism, be gone!" "Childlike explanations: grow up!" "Science and religion, forsake your destructive hostility: join hands and hearts!" We would rather attend your wedding, and, in the process, embrace a new world of discovery, wisdom, and love. Enjoy in these pages a dynamic, readable, and transformative experience, which will prove to be the unforgettable and broadening adventure of your daily and literary life.

We Christians have nursed on a life-long diet of traditions, laws, and teachings formulated through many hundreds of years. We learned them at the feet of parents, grandparents, priests, ministers, and teachers. We have trusted their truth and authority, and thus they have come to form the very marrow of our spiritual bones. Now, science and culture (including religious insights) are leaping forward, but many of us still cling to outdated dogmatic mandates.

We shall not present in these ten chapters new doctrines, nor refutations of the old, but updated understandings of the truths of our Christian tradition. They blend harmoniously with science, and strengthen powerfully the truths of our faith. Let us journey with courage into this new world where Christ still reigns. If we refuse this journey into today's world of all-encompassing love, who else will assume this pilgrimage? Truth and love need you now!

To conclude each chapter, we will pray to our beloved Lord within. These invocations will reflect the powerful messaging of that chapter. Because these pages represent such dramatic blending of our religious and scientific thinking, we will present an easy to understand summary of each chapter following the prayer.

Finally, the book forms an ideal text for classes and group discussion. Accordingly, you will find at the end of each chapter, questions not designed to test your knowledge, as to cause you to probe these supremely important subjects of 21st century science and religion. These discussions will challenge your minds, inspire your hearts, and energize your souls as God's intrinsic wisdom guides us in our dynamic journey into this new "promised land" of truth and enlightenment.

PRAYER

Lord God of all creation, we have failed to realize the immensity of you and your creation. Grant that these pages may help very many to view more accurately your prodigious role in each of us to bring about once again Eden on Earth through love in our hearts.
Amen.

1

PARTS & WHOLES

---

*To see a world in a grain of sand and a heaven in a wild flower;
holds infinity in the palm of your hand and eternity in an hour.*

WILLIAM BLAKE

*I do my thing, and you do your thing, I am not in this world to live
up to your expectations, and you are not in this world to live up to
mine. You are you, and I am I; if by chance we find each
other, it's beautiful. If not, it can't be helped.*

FRITZ PERLS

Fritz Perls, the noted twentieth century psychiatrist, developed the above Gestalt prayer in 1969 to encapsulate his approach to psychical therapeutics.

You are you, and I am I - each person stands alone and independently according to Perls, and each dies alone according to Soren Kirkegaard, a founder of Existentialism, who wanted his epitaph to read: "An individual." Some have applied this extreme individualism even to religion, so we often hear the very unchristian claim by some Christians, "I was saved on such and such a day." This, despite the fact that Jesus, their supposed hero, never spoke of his own personal salvation, but rather dreamed of a self-giving humanity.

As noted, nearly all of us, especially we of the West, view components of reality including ourselves, exclusively as individual parts. However, every part is also part of a more complex whole; as examples, a drop of water is part of the whole stream, which is part of the whole lake, which is part of the whole ocean, which is part of the whole Earth. Your arm is part of you; you are part of your society, which is part of all humanity, etc. Every individual human is part of a more complex physical whole which is a part of a whole reality.

My wife spent the whole year of 1978 weaving for me a tapestry of thirty-two square parts each about 2 inches by 2 inches with different shapes and colorful shades that comprise the whole, about 2 feet by 3 feet. It still hangs in our home and, when passing it, I think often of her commitment to me and its authentic relating of parts to wholes and our being parts of a societal whole.

Ilia Delio points this out: "As human beings and societies we seem separate, but, in our roots, we are part of an indivisible whole, and share in the same cosmic process."[1] Gary Zukav adds, "Our comfortable idea of a universe made up of solid little bits of matter behaving in logical ways has been exploded … The world is an interconnected tissue of events, a dynamic unbroken whole."[2]

The universal relationship of part to whole is not restricted to physicality. We need only consider the impact of artists and intellectuals whose work and achievements have flowed from others past and present. I truly acknowledge having borrowed precious wisdom

---

[1] Ilia Delio, *The Emergent Christ: Exploring the Meaning of Catholic in an Emergent Universe* (Maryknoll, NY: Orbis Books, 2011), 29.

[2] David Schiller, *The Little Zen Companion* (NY: Workman Publishing, 1994), 230.

from others in this very manuscript. We stand on the shoulders of our forebears: physically, intellectually, and spiritually. Don't we often hear someone say of a child, "He has the patience of his mother, or the courage of his father?" Our ancestors are part of us, and we become part of others to come. The poet reflects on this wholeness:

> *Nothing resting in its own completeness,*
> *Can have worth or beauty: but alone*
> *Because it leads and tends to further sweetness,*
> *Fuller, higher, deeper than its own....*
> *Life is only bright when it proceedeth*
> *Toward a truer deeper life above:*
> *Human love is sweetest when it leadeth*
> *To a more divine and perfect love....*
> *Nor dare to blame God's gifts for incompleteness*
> *In that they want their beauty lies; they roll*
> *Toward some infinite depth of love and sweetness,*
> *Bearing toward man's reluctant soul.*[3]

Because we reflect only rarely on our wholeness, we, as individual parts, have fallen into the trap of ghastly competition and even hostility with other parts. It's as if I must appear wiser, stronger or wealthier than you, although the opposite may be true on all three counts. Notice, for example, the frequency and severity of competitive religious wars: the extraordinary vitriol among today's politicians, the senseless struggle for monetary power, or the ongoing cultural hostility of East and West.

Several years ago while delivering a speech, I committed the unforgivable sin of mentioning possible future whole-world government, and was nearly booed and hissed off the stage by nationalists who

---

[3] Adelaide Proctor," Incompleteness," *A Little Treasury of Favorite Poems* (NY: Avenel Books, 1949), 313.

forget our nation is part of a greater whole: humanity. Ah! To realize that we are not just parts competing with each other! We are musicians blending harmoniously in the same orchestra, fashioning a synchronized whole melodic polyphony. This is not to say that we do not enjoy certain individuality, as with the first violinist in the orchestra, but he or she exists also as an essential part of the same greater whole.

We call beings that are simultaneously part and whole: holons. Because all of us are holons, we relate essentially to wholes and to other parts of wholes, all as parts of one final whole: reality. Therefore, you and I, however diverse we seem, are intimately bonded from the very core of our beings to the same whole. This negates the need for either of us to exceed or overpower another, for we are relatives, and belong to each other.

Humankind is one because we comprise one grand whole. We humans are bonded together to promote not just a part but the common good of the whole. We live with and for each other. David Grummett writes, "In a holistic world, each part of the world needs to be viewed with reference to the larger reality in which it participates."[4] We could even say you and I live to support each other part and the whole to which we all belong.

Paul likens us to members of one body each member of which is needed for the good of the whole.

> *God has put all the separate parts into the body ... If they were all the same part, how could it be a body? As it is, the parts are many but the body is one. The eye cannot say to the hand, 'I have no need of you, and nor can the head say to the feet, I have no need of you.* (1 Corinthians 12: 18-21)

We all need each other physically, psychologically, and spiritually for the good of our whole body. This wholeness destroys the rationale of the Christian who considers his/her faith superior to all others; or the radical Muslim who terrorizes other neighborly humans to receive his personal reward from a distant Allah; or the Jew for whom Adonai speaks not to all people as a whole, but only to his "chosen" people, the Jews. Such divisive walls explain fundamentally the depressing depravity of sin. Practical examples include: our apathy in accepting rank social injustice by ignoring the good of the whole human family; one's choosing maximum self-serving monetary profit at the expense of the whole or parts of the same whole.

One of many recent events illustrates the tragedy of disuniting the whole. It was January 07, 2015 in Paris, when terrorists murdered twelve people while shouting: "God is Greatest", and, "We have avenged the prophet Mohammed." Because of our unity in one body, such actions attack directly the whole of humanity including other Muslims. They and most of us don't understand and live our common wholeness and consequent close familial relationships.

---

[4] Ilia Delio, ed., *From Teilhard to Omega* (Maryknoll, NY: Orbis Books, 2014), 121.

We sin when we act out our hurtful perceptions of self, our brothers and sisters, or parts of the one whole creation. Therefore, we can describe sin as an attempt to hinder universal evolving into the truth and love of the whole. Sin comprises not only my personal failure but also my obstructing and offending the whole evolutionary process of God, humanity, and Cosmos.

Delio refers to Teilhard de Chardin by writing that religion is the occupation of all humanity individually and as a whole. Likewise, other living things, animals and plants seek their fulfillment (their sustenance and growth) by instinct as parts of the whole of nature. They thereby follow God's plan, and glorify God by their very identity in their relationships.[5] Delio quotes Thomas Merton:

> *A tree gives glory to God by being a tree. For by being what God means it to be, it is obeying God. It 'consents' to his creative love … Each particular being, in its individuality, its concrete nature, and entity with all its own characteristics [and relationships] … gives glory to God by being precisely what [God] wants it to be here and now.*[6]

Supposed inanimate objects also maintain their whole integrity and relationships, and therefore participate in this universal whole. Earth, the holon, abides also as a tiny part of the Milky Way, our spiral galaxy of about 400 billion stars and a greater number of planets. To gain a tiny idea of cosmic immensity, consider our nearest galaxy is Andromeda with over one trillion stars. These two galaxies are expected to smash together in about 3.75 billion years. Fortunately, you and I will likely not have to endure that collision of goliaths.

---

[5] Ilia Delio, *The Unbearable Wholeness of Being: God, Evolution, and the Power of Love* (Maryknoll, NY: Orbis Books, 2013), 9.

[6] Delio, *Unbearable Wholeness of Being*, 99-100.

Now consider these are merely two galaxies of more than 170 billion such galaxies- and these comprise only those we can observe or deduce, and such numbers continue to multiply. Earth becomes a miniscule ever-lessening speck in an ever-expanding Cosmos. In other words, the Cosmos now measures tremendously more than when I wrote these words. Each of us on Earth remains a tiny part of humanity, a proverbial "drop in a bucket," but the whole of humanity also represents the tiniest of minutiae in a mammoth whole series of oceans of created beings beyond number.

To summarize, we are immersed in a sea of holons. Examples are: rocks, clouds, and books that are wholes, but also parts of quarries, storms, and libraries. The Earth with all of us is a whole, but also part of an inconceivable whole munificent Cosmos of all created beings. Thus, Robert Furey describes humility as accepting our place in the universe, and that there is more to the universe than our merely physical eyes can see.

This entire evolving Cosmos with all its glorious bounty constitutes one wholly amazing whole. But, is this the ultimate whole? Certainly not! The ultimate whole must include God, (refer to chapter 2) in two ways. First, because God must pervade fully every created cell. Nothing except sin can be beyond God, and sin is our silly futile attempt to "play" God. God remains our origin, foundation, presence, and destiny. Second, God is present to the degree we (inspired by God) seek truth and love which is God.

Thus, God, within the cosmic, human, and Earthen creation, comprises the ultimate limitless whole of wholes from the least quark (fundamental subatomic unit) to the massive incredulous Cosmos with God as origin, soul, energy, and destiny of all that is. We discover God in all created beings and nowhere else. Finley quotes Thomas Merton,

> *Do we really choose between the world and Christ as between two conflicting realities absolutely opposed? No! It's not a question of either – or, but of all - in – one ... which finds the same ground of love in everything.*[7]

I recall being taught in the seminary to avoid or overcome the material world. Now, the tremendous truth! We find God in the material world and nowhere else Truly, we live in an axial age of a dynamic evolving relating process of parts and wholes.

This holistic world maximizes relationships among all its parts even to interdependence, one with the other. For example, infection of a single organ affects the health of the whole person; a weather system results from atmospheric and thermal change thousands of miles distant; an accident on a busy road will change the course and timing of vehicles, occupants, and so many others who are not even present. These multilateral relations include God who is constantly relating to us through our universal relatives in our beloved whole family called reality.

Believers can find God in all creation, but what of those who do not believe in God? Can they too discover God despite their own denial? Absolutely (pardon that word)! Both reasons still prevail: God certainly remains in every cell of their being on which we shall reflect in Chapter 2, and they do seek God albeit without their realizing it. Just as all the living, need and seek food for physical health whether we admit the need or not; similarly, we all need and seek truth and love (God) for our psychical and spiritual health whether we admit the need or not.

No human denies a truth she or he accepts, or denies genuine love of his or her self. Even Agnostics and Atheists who do not know or

---

[7] James Finley, *Merton's Palace of Nowhere* (Notre Dame, IN: Ave Maria Press, 1978), 57.

acknowledge God still seek what they perceive as truth and love, and that is God. Who can forget Augustine's classic aphorism, "You made us for yourself [Oh, Lord], and our hearts find no peace until they rest in you."[8] Panikkar writes: *"The human spirit is not satisfied with less than the whole."*[9]

Certain strands in the Judeo-Christian tradition have left us a dubious legacy by separating love of God from love of neighbor, and has thereby unwittingly divided love as a whole, into parts. Granted these strands "pay lip service" to one love of God and neighbor, but they have relegated love of neighbor to an inferior role by calling us to love primarily God in heaven. Despite Jesus telling us in Luke 10:28 that the two loves must be as one, many still believe these are separate loves.

Thus, many of us claim to love God, but hurl various epithets toward God's beloved: Christians, Jews, Jihadists, capitalists, gays, immigrants, atheists, and so called "others." Actually, there are no "others." If we don't love these imputed "others" as parts with God of our one whole family, we must recognize that, to that extent, we don't love God.

The horrific result of separating love of God and neighbor became clear in documents belonging to Mohammed Atta and his brother terrorists who attacked the Twin Towers September 11, 2001. These papers stated in part, "When boarding the plane, say: This raid is for Allah! Seconds before hitting the target, shout: There is no God but Allah!"

Many religious terrorists including Christians, Jews, Muslims and others commit their violence in terms of what they believe is truth and love in the name of Adonai, Allah, Christ, God; etc. The truth is

---

[8] Augustine, *Confessions*, trans., R.S. Pine-Coffin (NY: Barnes and Noble, 1992), 21.
[9] Panikkar, *Rhythm of Being*, 25.

that by harming you, I am harming Christ in you, and we have Calvary all over again. Will we ever learn to prioritize our holonic sisters and brothers over ideology?

Karl Rahner, the outstanding theologian, writes: "When one really understands the unity of the love of God and neighbor ... then we may safely say ... we have expressed the single totality of the task of the whole human being and of Christianity."[10] This oneness of love for God and all creatures beckons us to wholeness, and destroys fully and finally, religious, moral, racial, gendered, or any other justification for deliberate harm or hurt of self or any "other."

"God's in heaven and all's right with the world." This common phrase expresses egregious tragedy. We cannot and must not locate God in a distant heaven somewhere in the skies. Our God is not a sky-god. I affirm God is in you whoever you are, and you accept God in me whoever I am, despite whatever weakness or sin of which either of us bear guilt. We are all parts of wholes and the same ultimate whole. I, therefore, would never harm you; nor you, me, for God and we are parts of one whole.

From our standpoint, we are parts of the Earth and the whole Cosmos, and participate with our whole beings in this final ultimate whole: God, Cosmos, and humanity. One cannot imagine a more grand, profound, or complete whole: this remains the whole of reality. Our creating God of love, our incredible Cosmos including Earth, and we Earthbound, all join as one by love, for love, and in love.

Therefore, what fool would seek to terrorize God in God's beloved children especially when the perceived enemy and God and we are parts of the same whole we call reality? The whole objective for all

---

[10] Rahner, Karl, *The Love of Jesus and the Love of Neighbor* (NY: Crossroad Publishing, 1983), 84.

of us remains our growing love of self and all others in the whole Christ (cf Chapter 7). Our only task is discovering the most appropriate effective way to express our love.

Matthew Fox helped in 1979 to promote a scholarly discussion of what he called the web of creation. He quotes Fritjof Capra who quotes Albert Einstein as follows:

> *Quantum theory reveals a basic oneness of the universe ... nature does not show us any isolated 'basic building blocks' but rather appears as a complicated web of relations among the various parts of the whole.*[11]

Francis Thompson, the poet, beautifies this vision.

> *All things by immortal power, near or far,*
> *hiddenly to each other are, that thou canst not*
> *stir a flower without troubling of a star.*[12]

Fox continues, again quoting Capra,

> *In the new world view, the universe is seen as a dynamic web of interrelated events. None of the properties of any part of the web is fundamental [solitary]; they all follow from the properties of the other parts, [they all mingle] and the overall consistency of their mutual interrelations determines the structure of the entire web.*[13]

We therefore are bonded not only because of our functional mutuality in this web, but also structurally and therefore wholly. This includes obviously the human dynamics of science and religion, which have become tragically estranged but are now destined to become intimates in our grand human enterprise.

---

[11] Matthew Fox, *A Spirituality Named Compassion* (Minneapolis: MN, Winston Press, 1979), 144.

[12] Francis Thompson, "The Mistress of Vision," *The Oxford Book of English Mystical Verse*, Nicholson & Lee, eds, Oxford: The Clarendon Press, 1917) 644.

[13] Fox, Spirituality Named Compassion, 144.

Is there room for evil in our all-inclusive web? Surely so, and we will address it and Christ's spectacular epochal solution in Chapter 4.

One can trace the development of this thought from Matthew Fox's book thirty-seven years ago to that of Delio and others today. The latter employ their description of the web, but have plunged into greater depths by identifying and deepening the relational intimacy of beings as holons; that is, as parts and wholes of each other.

Additionally, these latter scholars complete the notion of the web by including, as we have seen, the Godhead itself as its bedrock, foundational to this all-inclusive whole and all its parts. We can literally say Earth, Cosmos, humanity, and God are all divinely, intimately, and wholly related, for, as Meister Eckhart remarks, *"God enters the soul with his all, not merely with a part; God enters the ground of the soul."*

As love, God seeks invincibly this amazing whole union with us. Therefore, we can now view more clearly that ultimate whole:

namely, our creating God of love fundamental to the whole exploding Cosmos, to Earth with its bounty, and to ourselves. This final ultimate reality compels us to an exquisite commitment to our God of love as experienced in each other, our mother Earth, and our all-embracing Cosmos.

Because our God of love pervades wholly all parts and wholes, we become whole only by loving; otherwise, we estrange ourselves, and drive ourselves into deserts of desolation, bereft of God and neighbor. How privileged we are to be and to belong to each other as parts and wholes and to the ultimate whole! Yes indeed, I love you, my God, in my brothers and sisters, Earth, and throughout a spectacular Cosmos. And, all of you love me because God resides incredibly throughout me.

We spoke earlier in this chapter of our resembling our parents. Now, we can understand that we, in our whole beings, image our divine parent, and additionally are becoming one with God to the extent we are accepting God (love) in our hearts. So, intended hurt of self or others becomes, as previously noted, wholly absurd! Fritz Perls states: "*I hear no longer your voice, only the sweet silence of one holonic family through all creation.*"

Someday, humanity will understand deeply and embrace passionately its own incarnational wholeness. Etty Hillesum did just that: she was the twenty-seven-year-old Jewish girl who, in danger of torture and death, helped to divert the shipment of many Jews from Auschwitz, the death camp. Finally, she felt compelled by her whole compassionate love to join her people there. The Nazis packed her into a cattle car September 7, 1943 with 1,000 others. These apparent captors shipped their soon-to-be martyred victims to Auschwitz, where they and the saintly Etty were gassed to death.

However, Etty was able to write the following words that have outlived the Nazis, and will indeed never die: "*I sometimes have the feeling that God is right inside me.... At such moments you are completely at one with the creative and cosmic forces that are at work in every human being, and ,,, are ultimately part of God.*"[14] T'was Etty, like the Christ, who was free; and the Caiaphas-like Nazis who, in their own chains, were captive; for the latter could no longer love, see, or touch their God, the loving God of a whole loving universe including the humanity they were torturing and murdering.

PRAYER

Lord God dwelling in all reality of every age, I join forever with the cosmic voices of stars, and bodies known and unknown. I connect with Mother Earth with her green, blue, and white beauty. I bond with Etty, and my sisters and brothers of all times and climes: the one hundred forty-four thousand. Together, as one mighty all-inclusive and thankful chorus, we sing and exult with you in
your consummate intimate presence.
Amen! Alleluia! Alleluia!

---

[14] Etty Hillesum, *An Interrupted Life: The Diaries of Etty Hillesum* (London: Jonathan Cape, Ltd., 1983), 62.

SUMMARY

Listen to the sweet sound of a symphony orchestra, and you will hear its varied sections merging to form a marvelous melodic theme. All the instruments contribute to the final rendition. So God, the universe, Earth, and humanity all lend their beings and becomings to comprise our astounding reality. That ultimate whole forever changes, nursing ever newly created scores.

The orchestra needs all its musicians, and if one plays off key, the whole harmony suffers. In our wondrous reality, you are needed to play your unique part in orchestrating the whole symphony. You are part of the orchestra, of the web.

GROUP DISCUSSION QUESTIONS

1. All objects are related – for example, a chair, a rose, a puppy, and a baby. How is that possible?
2. What is a holon?
3. How would society benefit from acknowledging its holonic existence?
4. Describe God as a holon.
5. Explain how an atheist seeks God unknowingly?
6. Matthew Fox and others describe reality as a web. What do we mean by that?
7. How could Auschwitz become a heaven?

2

OUR GOD OF WHOLENESS

There are only two ways; it seems to me, in which we can think about our existence here on Earth. We can agree with Macbeth that life is nothing more than a 'tale told by an idiot,' a purposeless embrace of life-forms .... Or we believe as Pierre de Chardin puts it, 'there is something afoot in the universe, something that looks like gestation and birth. In other words, a plan, a purpose to it all.'

JANE GOODALL

Sssh! Quiet! Slip into the silent spiritual depths of the core of your being beyond fear and death. But, don't pause there. Rather, plunge deeper beyond yourself, beyond all you know, into divinity. There, take your abiding rest in the serenity, certainty, and security of fulfilling love. Melt into love itself.

Ah! But we must return now! We must!

We Christians profess our faith in our God repeatedly with our lips. But, when you or I encounter the loss of a beloved, a heart-breaking divorce, addictions, financial ruin, or even life's daily trials, do we still retain faith in God's presence and love for us? Can we exclaim with the unknown father of Mark 9:24, "I have faith. Help my lack of faith!"

Even if we can say "yes", we still wonder about God and what she/he is really like, especially in light of the magnificent intersection of theology and science we have begun exploring. As we approach this confluence, we certainly must realize that, if we could understand God, we would thereby destroy God. God cannot exist within the severe limits of mere human rationality. Such thought is therefore not a valid argument for denial or acceptance of God. Still, humanity has need for an anchor, a sure foundation for truth and ethos.

If there is no God, reason is our only viable option, and thereby imprisons us in chains of logic. However, by human nature itself, we seek to fly freely, into the beyond. We are designed for boundless heights through terrestrial steps.

Church has for many centuries taught us that God exists as the uncaused cause, the omnipotent unchanging being who created all from nothing. However, we also accepted the biblical definition, that God is love. 1 John 4:16. But, we can't have it both ways. If God is unchanging, how can God be love, which is always seeking, thirsting, and embracing? On the other hand, if God is love, how can God be static, separate, and insensitive? Could God be a dynamic purposeful relationship, and not a being at all? We will explore this more deeply in Chapter 4.

Concerning the naked reality of God, my favorite evidence for her/his existence lies in the words of Teilhard de Chardin: "This is the point we must bear in mind: in no case could the Cosmos be conceived and realized without a center of a spiritual existence."[1] Panikkar explains further: Any and every man is inextricably linked with a world [his/her environs]; however, there seems to be a

---

[1] Ursula King, *Spirit of Fire the Life and Vision of de Chardin* (Maryknoll, NY:, Orbis Books, 1996), 113.

third element inseparable but also irreducible to the other two [the linkage itself]. One of its traditional names has been the divine, the deity, the Godhead.[2]

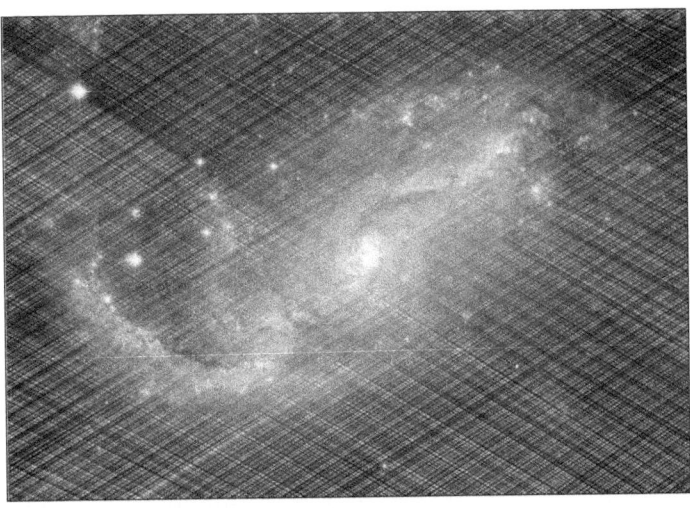

Paul Tillich, the astute theologian, provides metaphorical keys to unlocking the mystery of God's existing. We must, however, dismiss wholly and radically the idea of God as a separate being. Rather, Tillich, the theologian, considers God the *"depth" dimension of all reality*.[3] Experience in stillness the beauteous blue of the bird, the immensity of its dinosaural ancestors, the soft sound of a spring shower, the massive mystery of the oceans, the cosmic silence, and the heartfelt sweep of great music.

I remember clearly from my seminary days of yesteryear my silent experience of white. It was December 21, 1952 in Saranac Lake, NY. Another seminarian and I were happily assigned to venture out in a snowstorm to cut and retrieve a Christmas tree. As we began saw-

---

[2] Panikkar, *Rhythm of Being*, 211.

[3] Paul Tillich, *The Shaking of the Foundations* (London: Scribners, 1948), 52-63.

ing, the snow became so heavy we decided to postpone the task. So, we began our journey home.

Soon, the snow became a blinding "white-out", and we lost each other. Then it happened. This solitary halted in a world of gentle white caress, and realized the softening silent presence of the divine. I froze not because of the cold, but for fear of shattering the moment, and I vanished into the loving white whole. Soon, the snow lightened; I returned to myself, and resumed my journey, a changing young man as God nestled in my depths.

Many deny God because God's existence can't in their opinion be rationally proven. Actually, they fail to see before their very eyes the profound depths of God's loving presence in such exquisite union with created beings.

Bill Moyers, famed journalist, tells this illuminating story. Joseph Campbell, the renowned mythologist, overheard an American social philosopher say to a Shinto priest at an international conference on religion in Japan,

> 'We've been now to a good many ceremonies and have seen quite a few of your shrines, but I don't get your ideology. I don't get your theology.' The Japanese paused as though in deep thought and then slowly shook his head, 'I think we don't have ideology," he said "we don't have theology. We dance.'[4]

Likewise, Jean Paul Richter rhapsodizes, "God is an utterable sigh planted in the depth of the soul."[5]

Still, some question why we need a spiritual dimension of any kind. Why not accept what is visible or tangible and be satisfied? For ex-

---

[4] Joseph Campbell, *The Power of Myth* (NY: Doubleday, 1988), xxv.

[5] Jean Paul Richter, *God is Everywhere* (Kansas City: Hallmark, 1976), 9.

ample, Richard Dawkins, the famed biologist, (with whom many scientists disagree) says that evolution is merely the flow of genes striving for longevity. This will explain supposedly all of life's wonderings and searchings. Such thinking constitutes a form of literalism, refusing to question "why", or consider other valid options.

John Haught explains,

> *You ask, 'why is my car moving.' At one level of explanation, a good answer is 'because the wheels are turning.' At another level, an equally accepted explanation is that internal combustion has set the pistons, drive shaft, and so forth in motion. At still another level, the answer may be 'because Jim is driving it.'*[6]

Spirituality has on its level a legitimate right to its answer – particularly, when it does not offend other empirical explanations, and presents a powerful case for spectacular success. "The scientist asks how it works. The painter asks how it looks. The counselor asks how it feels. The mystic asks where it came from. And they all need each other."[7]

For Dawkins or anyone to dismiss a scientifically nuanced, wholly responsible theological explanation of reality in favor of an improbable, specious, negative rationale, breathes of a preconceived and perilous agenda. To deny God because I can't prove his existence is to live in hyperopia; that is, I can view distance but have difficulty seeing what's before my eyes. In contrast to Dawkins, the poet, Jean Favre, writes, "I do not believe in God for that implies an effort of the will – I see God everywhere."[8]

---

[6] John Haught, *Responses to 101 Questions on God and Evolution* (NY: Paulist Press, 2001), 57.

[7] Simon Parke, "Question Time", *Origins: For Those Bored With the Shallow End* (NY: Crossroad Publishing, 2001), 44.

[8] Harold Whaley, *God Is Everywhere* (Kansas City, Mo: Hallmark Cards 1976), 40.

I have a good friend, Danny, who is a recovering alcoholic. He and his family struggled to overcome his disease for twenty-two years. They tried counseling, interventions, physicians, and medications. All failed. Danny tried to take his life twice. The family of five suffered crushing heartbreak and financial ruin. Finally, he swallowed his pride, and again visited Alcoholics Anonymous with its Twelve Step Program. He had failed so many personal resolutions; he felt completely helpless, even a nothing.

Despite his lack of self-worth, Danny began to realize success because of his dependence no longer on himself, but on God's uniting with him. Indeed, six of the twelve steps spoke of God empowering him. His self-worth was reappearing in God, and he began walking past instead of into the Owl, his former favorite tavern. Danny has been sober for six years now, and attributes his abstinence to his love affair with his God. I trust Danny's witness more than Dawkins' stunted reasoning. Truly, God loves Danny, and each of us into new creation, as Dawkins himself has personally experienced.

Judy Cannato, scholarly author on theology and science, is referring to this implicitly when she writes,

> *If the universe had unfolded one trillionth of a trillionth of a percent slower, the gravitational force would have been too great and the universe would have imploded. If, however, the universe had unfolded one trillionth of a trillionth of a percent faster, matter would have escaped the gravitational pull, and the Cosmos would have flung apart ... It is [surely] not far-fetched to conclude there has been an intentionality toward life all along.*[9]

Do you remember Bette Midler singing those famous lines: "*God is watching us from a distance?*" This thinking presents a theological disaster. It forces us to conceive a distant God who creates and intervenes capriciously in the doings of creation. Similarly, when Einstein uses the image of "web" to describe creation, we can easily fall into a metaphorical trap by conceiving God's relationship to creation as that of a spider weaving its fibered creation. Such an image forgets that God, along with the whole Cosmos, Earth, and humanity, also comprise the web. God is one with the spider, but he's also one with the weaving and the web.

By following the theology we have been exploring, there can be no denying God's totally pervading presence through both the subject and the object and in their ever-changing relationships. This can be difficult for us, for, as noted previously, we have consumed a lifelong diet of God as a separate objective entity creating the Cosmos including humanity instantaneously and from nothing.

Rather, reflect on a pivotal moment in the life of the famed Joseph Campbell. He describes visiting Karlfried Durckheim, a wise German psychologist. Durckheim whispered, "The problem of life is to become transparent to transcendence so that you live in your life the

---

[9] Judy Cannato, *Radical Amazement* (Notre Dame, IN: Sorin Books, 2000), 9.

transcending divine life ... When this came into my vocabulary, it just seemed to be the only thing necessary."[10]

All this divine indwelling raises the question as to whether God is transcendent. With Durckheim, we answer, "yes!" However, that transcendence is not one of higher separateness but of unique intimate oneness with every cell, relationship, and experience. Simply speaking, God resides fully in every individual part, and whole, but also transcends every being by dwelling through every created being including ourselves.

Science informs that this Cosmos began with a "Big Bang" 13.7 billion years ago, and is still evolving. This "Big Bang" speaks of an event at that time so excessively hot and dense that it was expanding rapidly. As expansion occurred, temperatures cooled, and the first sub-atomic particles of energy formed. Obviously, this all-too-brief account of science and that of Genesis differ dramatically, and help to form the basis of the supposed irreconcilability of science and religion.

Delio, and others, however, resolve this apparent disconnect by describing the actual wedding of science and religion today by stating, "The story of the Big Bang **is** the new Genesis story, one that is awesome, powerful, filled with goodness and very old."[11] God is, by extension, **in** the big bang.

Remembering that God is energy, we recall the words of George Maloney: "In nuclear physics, we discover that everything material, possessing mass or quantity, is fundamentally energy. Such energy fields are in continuous and dynamic interacting relationships with

---

[10] Joseph Campbell, *The Hero's Journey* (Novato, CA: New World Library, 2001), 40.

[11] Ilia Delio, *The Emergent Christ, Exploring the Meaning of Catholic in an Evolutionary Universe* (Maryknoll, NY: Orbis Books, 2011), 6.

each other."[12] Panikkar writes: "[God dwells] inside and outside; the divine is immanent and transcendent. Many mystics say God wanders between us, inside and outside, goes in and out, appears and disappears, strays and dwells."[13]

We can look at this in another way: because God dwells in and through everything that is, there is nothing to which God is separate and external. God must be fundamental and one with all that is. Because God is energy, and we (indeed all creation) are energy, God and all creatures are radically linked. Imagine viewing a gorgeous garden in full bloom: roses, tulips, zinnias, etc., all blending in brilliant color. They are different, but they are all-floral, and, bonded in this created whole of divine beauty.

To expand on that image, all creatures are different, but all manifest divinity in a unique form of energy, and are thereby linked. O'Murchu writes, "*God is neither an entity in the world nor an entity outside it, but the revelatory - communicative - emancipatory - event - process - power by which the world is.*"[14]

Because love comprises the most powerful and worthy all-cosmic force, *God is love* (1 John 4:16). Our creating God consists of this energy of pure love and truth, into which we, also energy, are called to grow. John Duns Scotus, the unfortunately forgotten Franciscan theologian, addresses God summarily as the whole of what it means to exist.

Because of its own absence of limitation, God's love seeks to ban all restraints on the purity and universality of our love in our circumstances; that is, God is calling us to love in this moment fully as he/she loves. Jesus accomplished this in his circumstances, and so

---

[12] George Maloney, *God's Exploding Love* (NY: Society of St. Paul, 1987), 17.

[13] Panikkar, *Rhythm of Being*, 181.

[14] Diarmuid O'Murchu, *Evolutionary Faith*, 91.

models for us our exploding daily in our own continuous Big Bang of appropriate love for all God's beloved. Christ (cf. Chapter 7) calls us not just from the paradigm of his cross, but from his daily life and even from his empty tomb.

His message? That infinite love summons us to never-ending life now and forever in God and not to some grave. We can refuse this divine love, but God's self-offering can't be extinguished nor minimized. God's love leads and follows us everywhere, in every moment even from her/his burgeoning Big Bang. We are well aware of the marvelous mythic story of creation from Genesis, but, as we have seen, the story of the Big Bang is the story of the new Genesis. We shall explore this more deeply in chapter five. For now, we observe its truth, and give thanks for it.

Delio writes, "Franciscan theologian, Bonaventure, viewed creation not as an objective creation by a separate being but "as the outflow of divine self-giving love."[15] This inexorable, inexhaustible energy of love breathes forth ongoing creation from within the Big Bang and beyond.

We are as sounds or echoes of the Big Bang, and because God is one with the Big Bang, he/she is one with us. If we postulate divine creative action coming from the external (separate from the exploding Big Bang), God becomes an objective entity separate from creation and deciding to create or not to create, to love or not to love. Rather, God, love, is **compelled** to create, to overflow, by virtue of the very nature of love itself.

God is pre-cosmic love exploding in the whole Cosmos as dynamic relational love reaching out through the Big Bang and beyond to you, me, and all creation through multiparous persons, events, and worlds. Delio points precisely to this,

---

[15] Delio, *Emergent Christ*, 37.

> *For centuries, we have said 'God is love', and yet we have made God into something separate, static, and fixed. A fixed something cannot be dynamic love because love by its nature goes out from one to another to be for the other.*[16]

She adds, "God is not the separate static prime mover of a Cosmos but the dynamism of love welling up in space-time through the process of evolution and the rise of consciousness."[17]

There certainly is a Big Bang, but the Big Bang is the explosive power of supreme exquisite love energizing and expressing itself even materially in all creation. God is constantly overflowing into every created being. Thank you, God!

This divine love creates all creatures by manifest extension. You or I might travel to the depths of any ocean, or climb the highest peak, or fly to a celestial star and still, God, dynamic love, will embody us and all we touch. Even should we flee to the inner core of our own egoism, addiction, or malevolence, still we cannot escape God's consistent offerings of truth and love. This suggests the meaning of the mythic biblical tale of Jonah – each of us trying to flee futilely from accepting the love of God and the reciprocal challenge of loving divinely.

Thank God, we have no chance to escape God's offering of love because God's love for us remains utterly and eternally indestructible, as does our thirst for love. God, dynamic love, continues always expressing her/himself in every Earthen and cosmic body excluding sin, realizing thereby God's passion for a burgeoning universe of ever-deepening intimacy.

---

[16] Delio, Unbearable Wholeness of Being, 74.

[17] Delio, *Unbearable Wholeness of Being*, 74.

A terror-ridden corollary asserts that any resistance to this divine passion for universal love of a beloved constitutes sin: a traitorous betrayal of God, love, life, and universe. Therefore, Judas betrays not only Jesus but all of us and all creation, and our sin does the same. All sin seeks to disintegrate wholeness.

We have entitled our chapter "Our God of Wholeness." We can see now that this wholeness has two inseparable dimensions. First, wholeness consists of the entire purity of supreme love. Second, this divine love, God, lives in all created beings, and seeks necessarily to consume us wholly in its fiery conflagration. We recognize this in our innate desire to seek truth and love. Only Jesus, of all God's beloved children, has completely embraced God's fiery passion of love.

Hopefully, we spend our lives growing ever more closely to its caressing flames by his precious example. Understanding this wholeness of God summons us to live daily life to the fullest. God is one with our resting, rising, our autos, computers, pets, trees, and our joys and tears. God is not identical with us (pantheism), but is in divine union with us and all that is. We walk therefore in God's real Garden of Eden, and if we listen, we hear the echoes of God calling us from within all, to love without condition whomever and whatever we touch. This garden encompasses all creation in continuing liturgical celebration. It is God rejoicing in this magnificence of union crowned by humanity's free choice to sing evermore fully the melody of divine ecstatic love.

Philosophers and sages have struggled through all time with one seemingly powerful objection to this wholeness of divine love. "How can a God of love perpetrate or allow horrific evil to be inflicted on innocent humans?" No one seems to have the answer to this problem of evil. Even Pope Benedict XVI cried out in May 2006 at Auschwitz "In a place like this, words fail; in the end, there can only be a dread silence which itself is a heartfelt cry to God: 'Why Lord, did you remain silent? How could you tolerate all this?'"[18] It's as if Benedict considers God recoiling from such horrific evil in horror, unable to address it.

Viewing God in this humanistic objective way suggests God and we have no answer to this monumental question. That can't be! God, love, is more powerful than evil! God, truth, is more knowing than ignorance. We suggest that Jesus, the face of divine love on Earth, has understood and solved this problem of the ages with his teaching and especially with his life of surpassing union with all daughters and sons of God.

Why does Jesus not receive credit for his magnificent solution; because we humans have been unable to understand and unwilling courageously to embrace it. God did not recoil from the Zyklon jets of Auschwitz or the ovens of today's madness. Rather, God, in eve-

---

[18] Jim Manney, *The Best Catholic Writing* (Chicago: Loyola Press, 2007), 81.

ry victim, breathed this murderous gas and was consumed in the ovens with and in his beloved.

In Chapter 4, we will further explore the faith-filled astounding solution of Jesus to this previously insoluble problem of evil.

We observe that we spring from, live in, and aspire to the boundless love that only God can offer. We swim in a limitless ocean of Godness amidst God's presence in all. Despite the horrors of today's carnage, yesterday's ovens, and the horrendous injustice inherent in human life, we will see in Chapter 4 that evil does not trump love. What we calculate often as evil consists of our inability to understand what priceless intimacy with God means and the inexpressible numinous union to which God invites us. Get ready for Jesus' answer to this apparently insoluble question of the ages.

George Maloney writes of this identifying love with God:

> *Brother Lawrence, the 17th century Carmelite brother who practiced so faithfully the presence of the indwelling trinity ... writes: "The deeper and more intimate you are with him, the*

greater will be your love for him. And if our love for the Lord is great, then we will love him as much during grief as in joy ... Oh, dear friend, the Lord is not outside you, pouring down favors; the Lord is within you. Keep him there, within."[19]

We remember that God, love, resides not only in us but in every being. Every being is therefore sacramental; all is sacrament.

Some years ago, my daughter, Joy, loved desperately a young man named Dan. However, he suffered amyotrophic lateral sclerosis disease (Lou Gehrig's disease), in which the patient suffers progressive loss of muscle mass and function. She accompanied him for years in his pain and grief in this downward spiral of agony until his cruel death. Would she become embittered? Would she turn with blame on God?

Joy still grieves, but is coming slowly to realize that she herself still redounds with life and possibilities as part of the whole. Today, she wishes she had never had to endure such suffering, but she also understands more clearly the supreme unchallenged value of their love. Further, Joy knows that dying is a part of that whole called life, the purpose of which is to grow in love, in God. To grow in love is to evolve as a created human person into oneness with love (God) now and forever. This defines our success as human beings. True, many of us are "hung up" on money, control, and self-seeking, but it is self-giving in love that truly measures our greatness and joy now and forever.

The ultimate evidence of our love is neither prayer, nor penance, nor following certain rules nor doctrines, nor intellection of itself (all excellent), but primarily living God's life as Jesus lived it. We

---

[19] George Maloney, *Called to Intimacy, Living in the Indwelling Presence* (NY: Alba House 1983), 50.

can never return God's love for us adequately, but we can spend our lives entering ever more deeply in communion with God in our beloved creation.

PRAYER

Lord God, we know you reside as love in the depths of our hearts and of all creation. Our union with you empowers us to live your life of love. Grant us therefore the resolution and courage to love to the fullness of our capability in your image, so that no pain, not even death, can cause us to betray our commitment to progress   in our Earthen journey to wholeness.
Amen.

SUMMARY

Theologians have long considered God as the uncaused cause who created from nothing. This, however, renders God a separate being, and God is not separate from anything. Rather, God is within everything and outside of nothing. God is relationship; in particular, God is the relationship of love within all parts and wholes of creation. We cannot capture God by reasoning to God's existence.

Rather, God is before our very eye – in creation transparent to his/her transcendence. We "see" God only with a third eye that sees through the mundane. Creation thus derives not from God creating from nothing, but from God (love) exploding. This is the Big Bang which sounds through all. This does not deny evil, but overcomes and outlasts – as we will see in Chapter 4.

GROUP DISCUSSION QUESTIONS

1. Is God love or the uncaused cause (the first cause)?
2. Can we really "prove" God's existence?
3. How can God be transcendent if present in created beings?
4. How do Adam and Eve relate to the Big Bang?
5. Why is it important that God was compelled to create?
6. What is the ultimate whole?
7. Is God a being within us?

3

LIVING IN THE TRINITY

The Trinity is not a dogma to be taken literally, but a primordial truth of universal, symbolic significance. It was a human attempt to describe a core value (or set of values) of the God we Christians believe in – namely, relationality.

DIARMUID O'MURCHU

Do you understand the Trinity? Neither do I. Nevertheless, this mystery lies at the very heart of Christianity, and thus calls for our exploring it deeply. Because it is the least understood explains why it is also the most ignored, and the reverse is just as true. Actually, the Trinity helps immeasurably our understanding cosmic theology. So, with your deeper appreciation of the Trinity, it is about to assume new dynamic importance in your spiritual life.

We saw in Chapter 2 that God lives in and through every being of the created whole from the sub-atomic quark to the boundless Cosmos. Our conclusion? The triune God lives therefore in every being and to the degree it accepts our God of love.

Although the scriptures of the first century never explicitly mention Trinity as such, Christian theologians have been discussing its meaning ever since. Clement of Rome refers to it in his Letter to the Corinthians about 96 CE, and later, the Councils of Nicaea 325 CE and Constantinople 381 CE. The doctrine quickly became fully accepted as fundamental to Christian faith. Despite these deliberations and many others through the centuries, we must acknowledge the life of the Trinity has remained a profound mystery.

This being said, theologians are able to distinguish the life of the Trinity into those *immanent* relations among the three persons within God's life and the *economic* ties that refer to the presence of God in the world of creation.[1]

This distinction of immanent and economic may be likened to the Sun with its inner nuclear explosions and its rays, which warm and nourish us Earthen travelers. Both are identical with the latter representing the extension of the former; that is, the immanent and economic dimensions of Trinity identify with each other in intensity, universality, and longevity. These two, immanent and economic, must identify, for God, unlike us, does not admit of varying intensity.

Karl Rahner, one of our greatest twentieth century theologians, adds, "*The economic Trinity is the immanent Trinity, and the immanent Trinity is the economic Trinity.*"[2] Therefore, the triune God offers herself/himself fully and appropriately to every created being. This bears momentous significance for us in that the Trinity dwells within us in all its **full** love, compassion, and truth. This "over the top" love of God burns within, seeking to impassion us as it did Jesus.

---

[1] Richard McBrien, *Catholicism*, Study Edition, (Minneapolis, MN: Winston Press 1981), 90.

[2] Karl Rahner *The Trinity* (Freiburg, Germany: Herder and Herder, 1970), 22.

Those who suffer depression or lack of self-esteem can distrust themselves, but there is no distrusting the triune God who courses throughout their entire beings with consummate union.

Christians! All humanity! Why, depression? Our betrayals, addictions, and apathy provide opportunities for greater union with God whose love for us can't be lessened by whatever our failings. If we seek Trinity sincerely, within self and all created beings where God actually lives, we find our God.

Because in the past, we have framed Trinity as a separate, remote, and thoroughly ethereal doctrine, it's not surprising that most Christians have displayed little or no interest in Trinity. However, for you, that is about to change! For unlike the Sun, the Godhead lives within you: the Father constantly creating you; the Son saving you; and the Spirit cherishing you. These form the breath of God, sending you forth as the Lord's official ambassador carrying this Christly good news to all you touch.

Let's imagine God considering whether she/he will create or not create, sustain or not sustain. God weighs options, and arbitrarily comes to a fortunate decision in creating us. Is this the creative God in whom you and I place our trust? Not hardly! May the true God of living reality save us from this whimsical God of childhood, from a divinity with the possibility of creating or not, sustaining or not, or, heaven forbid, changing his/her mind.

This scenario pictures the separate, objective, and arbitrary God we worshipped since childhood, and to which we referred in Chapter 2. It projects on divinity the manner in which we humans arrive at our decisions: by considering arguments for and against, discerning their comparative value, deciding, and effecting. God, however, is certainly not human in this sense, and definitely not arbitrary. We naively apply our mode of reasoning to God, the supreme love-energy of the entire Cosmos. How dare we! The truth is that God does not arrive at a decision by deliberation. Rather, God is driven (compelled) by the purity and ardor of her/his own love, to love.

We have traditionally looked on Trinity as one separate God in three distinct persons. This is spiritual myopia. Panikkar explains,

> *The main insight of the doctrine of the Trinity is simple. Ultimate reality [God] is neither one [being or substance] with three modes [of expression], nor three [beings or substances] within a single abstract oneness. The Trinity is pure relationship, and here lies the great challenge and the profound transformation. If the divine were a substance, we would have three Gods; if the divine is infinite relationship, this relationship immerses all creatures and [humanity] in a special way.*[3]

As adult searchers, we can no longer think of God as a wise heavenly person or any substantial being but only as relationship, the relationship of radical love. Each relationship, whether within the immanent or economic Trinity, differs from the others not in quality or intensity, nor in any other distinguishing standard, but only because they are different relationships; for example, as a father, I love my three children with equal intensity, but the relationships remain distinct. Each relationship of the economic Trinity is and always will remain as the fullness of love but is still distinguished. God relates to **you uniquely** in all creation with the fullness of divine love.

No one can relate to God as you do. No one ever will. God loves you as God will never love anyone. Therefore, when reflecting on the Godhead, we do not look to a person in heaven, but to the intensity, catholicity, (universality), and endurance of the relationship of pure love radiating in us and in all created beings. As our love for God in each created being grows, God grows in us and becomes

---

[3] Panikkar, *Rhythm of Being*, 225.

newly born on Earth. God becomes incarnate in each of us all over again.

Reflecting on **inner** Trinitarian life, Delio draws from Bonaventure by stating:

> Love is based on three closely related Trinitarian terms: primacy, fecundity [fruitfulness], and communicability: [creator, savior, and inspirer]. (These three do not only derive from selection by the early church, but describe summary and effectively the origin and action of love). The first divine person, the Father, he [Bonaventure] writes, is without origin, and is primal and self-diffusive, the source or fountain-fullness of goodness. The Son is that person eternally generated by the Father's self-diffusive goodness ... that is, the Father naturally and necessarily [communicating] goodness out of the fountain-fullness of goodness ... The Son/Word, is generated by the Father, and with the Father; the [Father and] Son breathe forth the Spirit who is that eternal bond of love between the Father and the Son.[4]

Merely speaking of these three persons presents the danger of conceiving of three separate entities, and prioritizing the Father before the Son and Spirit. Not so. We must remember God is the relationship of love in the form of creating, saving, and inspiring among and in all created beings.

These pages describe our God evolving from a Grecian first cause of being to a blazing postmodern relational fury of love trying to rise in every beloved unique child. Perhaps, you remember the Sherwin Williams Paint Company using as a logo a picture of a small Earth with red paint coursing down over its surface. This analogy of God works up to a point, but the paint covered only the surface.

---

[4] Delio, *Emergent Christ*, 37.

God, however, engulfs deliberately the entire Cosmos and not just the surface, but in it, through it, and all through us: God, pervasive love, and foundational Spirit. Thus, the key to enlivening the Trinity in our lives is to realize profoundly that the divine Trinity of the whole Earth and Cosmos identifies himself/herself by living and loving fully in each of us: in you.

Consider this amazing corollary: that the God of supreme love relationship through all time and space is calling you and me to replicate in our lives the Trinity's surpassing love in our relationships. The author of Ephesians writes: "As God's dear children, then, take him as your pattern, and follow Christ by loving as he loved you." (Ephesians. 5:1) Jesus exclaimed: "I have loved you just as the Father has loved me." (John 15:9)

Love, of its essence, reaches out to another, and thus Delio writes: "The Father expresses himself in the Son, [and the Son in the Father]. This self-expression is the basis of the infinite word of God and all finite existence as well."⁵ We creatures are, because God is. God's exploding love, the Holy Spirit, expresses godliness in every corner and crevice of creation uniquely. God is in love with every part of us and the whole of us! Are we in hostility with each other, indifferent with each other, or are we in love with each other?

Finally and incredibly, God calls us by her/his union with us to continue God's eternal and cosmic love into every niche. This was the proclamation of Jesus. Andrew Greeley had it right many decades ago: "They refused to listen to what he [Jesus] was saying ... because it was too spectacularly good, much too good; in fact, too good to be true."⁶

The term "presence of God" rings familiar to most Christians, but hopefully we understand this not in terms of an objective presence to us or inside us, but rather by the Trinity's "pervading" every cell and intimation of the Cosmos, Earth, and each of us. Whoever or whatever we experience informs us of the Father's creating, the Son's redeeming, and the Spirit's inspiring us to greater heights of wholeness (holiness).

Delio quotes Panikkar: "The whole of reality [and each part including each of us] could be called: Father, Christ, and Holy Spirit – The font of all reality."⁷ This is a towering insight, and wholly transformational in our world-view and behavioral motivation. The Trinity becomes my grounding, yours, and that of every Earthen and cosmic creation. And this has extended (evolved) from and through the Big Bang unto this moment and beyond. No one could imagine a more amazing vision of reality and our participating in it.

---

⁵ Ilia Delio, *Christ in Evolution* (Marynoll, NY: Orbis Books 2008), 59.

⁶ Andrew Greeley, *The Jesus Myth* (Garden City, NY: Image Books 1971), 54.

⁷ Delio, *Christ in Evolution*, 91.

We experience reality continuously, and yet routinely fail to see its divine depths. Because we don't recognize it, does not mean our triune God of love does not continue to love us, through all created beings and experiences of our lives. The poet, Simon Parke, writes with an insightful eye:

> *As any desert-dweller will tell you, when looking for firewood among the big sands – and you will need to, for it's very cold at night – you should look <u>beneath</u> the sand where the wicked wind has buried it. Dig down! Just because you don't see it on the surface, doesn't mean it isn't there. If you want to keep warm amid the cold, dig down!!*[8]

With rich meaning, Jesus exclaims to the Pharisees: "I have come into this world so that those without sight can see." (John 9:39) Now we know why Teilhard entitles his book The Divine Milieu, in which he writes: "The man with a passionate sense of the divine milieu cannot bear to find things about him obscure, tepid, and empty which should be full and vibrant with God."[9] The opacity of some makes for a life dull and boring, while true insight drives our lives with depth, marvel, adventure, and insightful passion.

Our whole lives consist in recognizing and living God's gracious universal pervasion in more and more of our beings, relationships, and experiences. God is calling us to see Trinitarian fullness in all. A fountain of love, its grand moment-to-moment expression, and the activating inspiration of love await birth in our conscious transformation. The Cosmos, our Earth, its living, and nonliving chil-

---

[8] Simon Parke, "Desert Warm", *Origins*, 10.

[9] Teilhard de Chardin, *The Divine Milieu*, trans. by William Collins (NY: Harper and Row, 1960), 144.

dren, all join with our hearts in seething with Trinitarian indwelling.

So, God is calling us to view with a third eye her/his abiding in all creatures! So many so-called "people of God" fail to see his innate Trinitarian presence because of their shallow literality, and, even worse, then pretend to speak for Christianity. On a lighter note, you may recall Sir Arthur Conan Doyle's master sleuth, Sherlock Holmes, berating his close but obtuse friend Dr. Watson: "Watson, you see, but you don't observe!"

As we grow in recognizing, accepting, and living this wondrous Trinitarian grace, we walk more and more in the sandals of Jesus. He became the Risen Christ, and we tread the same path to experience the same destiny. Living this identity makes us a Christ, and constitutes a contemplative life. This is possible for all of us, and comprises the reason Thomas Merton called everyone, not just monks, to lead a life of contemplation, of seeing these divine depths, and living in such heartening love, moment to moment.

When we shape, save, or inspire any created beings, we are acting as co-creators with God, for this is what God has been doing for 13.7 billion years. Our cooperative action with love (God) requires our care and embrace of all creation: living and nonliving, Earthen and cosmic, material and spiritual, and especially human. The bishops of Appalachia issued in 1995 a letter, *At Home in the Web of Life,* in which they described a sense of awe before creation that reveals the loving face of the creator and implores our care of precious Earth today as God's second Eden.[10]

We journey en route from the Eden of bitter disappointment to the Eden of joyous care-giving. Because God continues to create, maintain, and beautify creation through us, we are co-creating literally his/her cosmic and Earthen bounty, today's Eden. We seek especially to save our compatriots in life here and forever, and to inspire others in this privileged divine tasking. We thus repeat in our daily lives the whole work of the Trinitarian God within all. Have you ever dreamt your life could be so meaningful, so heavenly, so divine?

We must be wary of accepting as pure gift God's Trinitarian presence. We have been so expertly trained to view God as "out there" that even the word "presence" could be easily misunderstood as objective and separate. Delio refers to Donald Gray by stating:

> *Teilhard opposed the idea of an absolutely gratuitous creation that makes creation independent of God or merely contingent on God. This type of radical dependency of creation upon God diminishes the significance of the world in relation to God. Creation is not merely gift of God; it is being-in-love with God. It's more than an act willed out of intellect or desire ... God is not supernatural*

---

[10] *http://ccappal.org/publications/pastoral-letters* (accessed 2017-08-31).

being from above, but the supernatural center of everything that exists.[11]

In our next chapter, we shall probe the immensity of this love, and the union it generates.

We have previously acknowledged God's foundational presence in all created beings; now we realize this as Trinitarian presence, and it's bonding together all creation. Panikkar carries it further:

"There are no such things as God or man or world considered as completely independent entities. Not only are they dependent on one another, but this dependence is structural; that is, constitutive of their being. Panikkar coins the term 'interindependence' to express this relationship.[12]

God breathes her/himself into all beloved beings. We belong to each other ideally, as the three persons of the Trinity belong to each other. The Trinity is calling each of us to be a divine extension and expression of divine love even as the ray of the sun flows from its solar source. Our God is creating us to live our human lives on Earth in the spirit of immanent Trinitarian love. This calling comprises the greatest and most august role humanity has or ever will receive.

This exquisite insight achieves its true value only when it leads to transformed living by our evolving ever more fully into God's Word today, the Risen Christ. The Trinity will come alive in us insofar as we live God's life of love. We remember that all beings are holonic outgrowths of the same root, and that root is divine love. This perception by itself ought to strike a blow at the hearts of all forms of

---

[11] Delio, op cit., *The Unbearable Wholeness of Being*, 69.

[12] Joseph Prabhu, Foreword, *The Rhythm of Being* by Raimon Panikkar (Maryknoll, NY: Orbis Books 2010), xviii.

discrimination, violence, boredom, and exploitation. It brands these ultimately as affronts to God and all created reality.

Thomas Berry perceives this self-indulgence in a similar way:

> *We need to avoid that anthropocentrism [arrogance of human superiority] that would make [humanity] so absolutely the norm of value that we fail to recognize that the larger concern must be for a universe that includes the human, but is a greater reality than the human.*[13]

We conclude this chapter by realizing (seeing with real eyes) the heartbeat of Trinitarian love pulsing through the eons of space and time, through every created being, to ourselves, and all our experiences, and beyond. Truly, we breathe the rarefied air of the divine.

PRAYER

> *Oh, holy and three-fold dynamic lover, we are grateful for your continuing incarnate presence in us and your cosmic creation. We thank you especially for our unique human gifts and your sharing with us your creative role. We resolve to think your thoughts, walk in your passionate presence, and live your life of wisdom in the example of Jesus. In a word, continue to teach and inspire us to co-create with you our whole world into your whole beauty.*
> *Amen.*

---

[13] Berry, *Teilhard in 21st Century*, 31.

SUMMARY

Because we know and affirm God's living in all of us, therefore, the Trinity lives within us. Amazingly, the whole and every part of reality is filled with Trinitarian pregnancy. Those who see only what's visible are seeing only what's apparent. We are co-creators, co-redeemers, and co-lovers with God to all created depths. The divine Trinity is actually calling us to live with the same relationship as that of divine immanent love. There can be no human calling to equal these celestial heights. Understanding, accepting, and living this, creates Eden, again, only this time for real.

GROUP DISCUSSION QUESTIONS

1. Why do theologians assert God is three persons?
2. If God is neither one being nor three, what is God?
3. What does divine pervasion mean?
4. Why are you a contemplative?
5. Why did God not create from nothing?
6. Describe your interdependence.
7. Why is humanity simply a part of creation and not its master?

4

ABOUNDING LOVE

Love is the most universal, the most tremendous, and the most mystical of cosmic forces. It is like the blood of spiritual evolution.

Teilhard de Chardin

I am certain you're too young, but unfortunately for me, I can remember a hit song from many years ago entitled "Love Makes the World Go Round." Its title says it all.

By creating, saving, and inspiring every being throughout the universe, our treasured Trinity more than fulfills the song's promise, and becomes our communal and personal lover within each of us and all that is. This awe-filled insight informs us that we have no enemies, only beloved. Nonetheless, too many of us have "bought a bill of goods" sold by too many politicians, militarists, economists, and opportunists who claim that one's own self, church, university, nation, army, etc. must be number one. This culture mandates that we surpass our neighbor.

However, the Trinity does not consist of three-way competition, but rather three-way communion, and calls us to replicate such in our lives by creating, expressing, and inspiring others in Christ. Neither defeating nor eclipsing our neighbor becomes our objective; serving her/him and defeating hostility itself becomes our goal.

God calls us to wage war not against any person or community; but only against God's enemies: violence, apathy, and hostility themselves. If we insist on competition, then such competition ought to answer the question, "How can I love more fully, more humanely and divinely than yesterday?"

Every created being is unique. Every cosmic and Earthen event, every planet, and animal, every snowflake or raindrop has its own contour, consistency, location, and relationships. We humans, like all creatures, are distinguished by congenital and relational impacts. You and I, as sister and brother holons, form distinct parts of the same wholes, but we remain unique.

Joan, my wife, and her sister remain identical twins, but their physical, psychological, and spiritual differences distinguish them clearly. All this originality provides breathtaking opportunity for God's love to manifest itself through each of us in ways beyond number and shape with our every moment-to-moment relationship and experience.

Because love creates us, we can state literally that we are formed by, for, and in love. Love remains our divine DNA. As we explored in Chapter 3, we live among dear and intimate family members bonded by God's Spirit of love in and from all of us. We can illustrate this by picturing the extraordinary familial love Jesus displayed for his whole human family, who "hear the word of God and keep it." (Luke 11:28)

In a word, Jesus loved appropriately all beings with all his heart. Such love applies to all in whom God dwells; to a sparrow searching for food, a wave caressing a beach, or a mother nursing her babe. Every experience in all nature expresses in some way divine love. It's not surprising the poetic soul of Francis of Assisi sings of this in his mystical hymn of harmony, *The Canticle of the Sun*

> *Through sister moon and the stars....*
> *Through brother wind, and air and clouds*
> *and storms and all the weather through*
> *which you give your creatures sustenance....*
> *Through those who forgive for love of you.*
> *Praise and bless my Lord and give thanks.*
>
> St. Francis in Sunny Meadow.

Francis was absorbed with our God of supreme love and togetherness. He and we would not give our lives for a God who was aloof, cold, and arbitrary, despite church often teaching that God ruled with foreboding omnipotence in heaven. Rather, his God and ours, touches affectionately our hearts and entire beings with a presence of unbounded intimacy and union.

Genuine love exists today among us as an endangered species. I truly believe there has never been in human history, more words written and spoken about love with less meaning. The word love falls easily from our lips but with exceeding difficulty from our heart. Entrepreneurs, sexual partners, religious leaders, spouses, and others express their love with ease, but who has the courage to live in full commitment to another. Even our repetition of the word, love, in these pages risks losing the passionate and sacrificial devotion of genuine love.

Delio writes:

> *Love has been consigned to emotion and sentiment, emptied of any real power and thus a thing for play. Modern culture's preoccupation with the physical body and its exploitation as soulless matter, reflects the deep human disconnect from self, neighbor, Earth, and God. Sex has become more like a video game with the thrill of winning rather than part of the deep core of cosmic evolution.*[1]

Mindful of our cultural betrayal of love, we ask earnestly, "What is love?" Scott Peck responds, "Love is the will to extend one's self for the purpose of nurturing one's own or another's [physical, psychological, or] spiritual growth."[2] We can and must expand his definition to include God who is love, for it is love that initiates and holds together reality, the ultimate whole. Further, love drives reality forward in its endless search for greater comprehensive and profound love.

Picture the most trusted love of your life: your spouse, child, parent, friend, or significant other. Now, picture him or her who has hurt you the deepest. Like God, you and I are called to love both fully. Our expressions and applications of love would differ appropriately, but our responses must spring from love. Hopefully, our love would fulfill the three requisites that Peck expresses in his definition.

- *First:* your love must lead to **action**; promises and words of themselves, no matter how sweet, fail the test. We see this in so many relationships; for example, a bride and groom pledge their abiding love "until death do us part." Then, too often, this apparently genuine commitment withers quickly midst the challenges of life's storms. Many years ago, my grandmother

---

[1] Delio, *Unbearable Wholeness of Being*, 50-51.
[2] M. Scott Peck, *The Road Less Traveled* (NY: Simon & Schuster 1978), 81.

pointedly informed this small boy, "Actions speak louder than words," and he never forgot *it*.

- *Second:* according to Peck, true love seeks the physical and spiritual growth of the beloved; that is, it includes and reaches through the physical to the spiritual core of our humanity. The wife of an alcoholic came to my office for counseling not because of her husband's drinking, but because she, in mistaken love, was acceding to his Friday pleadings to purchase liquor for his consumption every weekend. She was as ill with co-dependency as her husband with alcoholism, and in the name of love, was enabling him. The lover must ask the question: "Is my behavior truly helping my beloved to live a better life?"

- *Third:* despite certain obvious human rejections, in every era, divine love has proven incredibly fertile throughout the whole Cosmos, and lives in us to nourish that fertility. The true lover calls her/his beloved not to rest in a destructive comfort zone, but to rise from it, and address the challenges of new relationships and new life, often in an uncomfortable zone.

Tough love is real, and at times, necessary, as I learned from my father many years ago. Love supports "the other" even to sacrifice of self. However, the "other" can include love of one's self, for the ability of self-reflection (seeing self as an "other") distinguishes and highlights us humans. In this way, self becomes a beloved other.

An astonishing insight sees God as love so united with genuine human love that they can't be separated to distinguish otherness. Gary Zukav concludes that "eventually you will come to understand that love heals everything and love is all there is."[3] Indeed, could love comprise the ultimate whole, and become the foundation upon which all healthy religions find their oneness?

---

[3] Gary Zukav & Linda Francis, *The Mind of the Soul* (NY: Simon and Schuster), 106.

Most people would agree that a human's most exalted and challenging act is loving, but love also plays a key role in the world of philosophy. The science of metaphysics studies traditionally "being" as most fundamental to all beings. Some (for example, Thomas Aquinas following Aristotle) identify God as being, itself. However, Delio and many others argue convincingly that being is "intrinsically relational;"[4] that nothing including God exists autonomously, that is, without relationship. I recall the story of a wealthy man in Maine who built a completely, soundproof tower without light or any sensory stimulation so he could experience total isolation. Then, after a time, he refused to enter because of the absence of sensory relationships and love.

Relationship necessitates energy so that all, from miniscule quarks to humanity to Cosmos to God, comprise fields of energy. We call God's field of energy, exploding love, with which God creates and energizes all his/her children. You and I might well ask ourselves, "What is my field of energy?" Most of us have an image of God as an objective ruler who lives in heaven, but a postmodern, genuine, and relevant Christianity teaches God is not a person or being.

Bede Griffiths proclaims, "*God is interpersonal communion, a communion of love which is in all of us, and embraces us all as the real meaning of our lives.*"[5] That metaphysics which asserts being itself is most fundamental to all beings is clearly inadequate, for all that exists, is relational not inert being. Teilhard asserts,

> *Let us therefore try to replace a metaphysics of "Esse" [being] with a metaphysics of "Unire" [to unite] .... This participated being would be defined not so much by its opposition to non-being*

---

[4] Delio, *Unbearable Wholeness of Being*, 45.

[5] Bede Griffiths, *The New Creation in Christ* (Springfield, IL: Templegate, 1992), 18.

*as by its positive relation to God, [to ultimate love] its power of entering into communion.*⁶

Divine love, overflowing and inflowing through every being, is ultimately foundational, as we have noted, to the structure and function of every being, physical, spiritual, or experiential. "*As long as we love each other, God remains in us and his love comes to its perfection in us.*" (1 John 4:12) We either choose to live in this warmth of love or languish in the bitter cold of its absence.

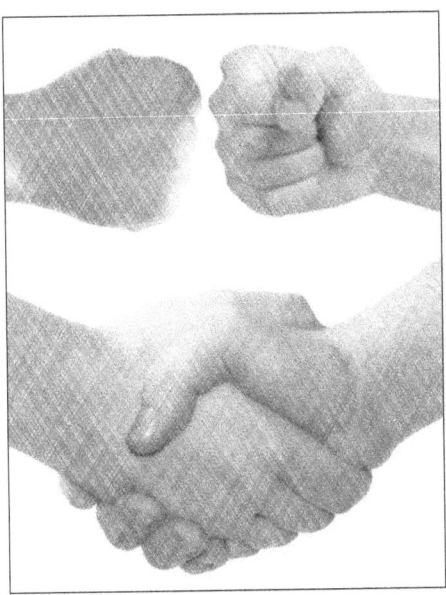

One could object to this thinking of the totality of love as being "way out there;" naïve, idealistic, while questioning: "Why do you refuse to acknowledge the presence of so much evil in our world?" Much evil arises from our own human failings, but it's true, we must admit there are disasters beyond our control, flowing seemingly from God. Some insurance companies even dare to excuse an accident as an "act of God."

---

⁶ Teilhard de Chardin, *Christianity and Evolution*, (NY: Harcourt and Brace, 1969), 227.

I think of my friend, an inmate on death row, who was not even in the town where the vicious murder occurred, or a stillbirth, (as my wife and I experienced twice). Such extremely painful events do occur, and surely, an all-knowing and all-powerful separate deity could, according to this outdated thinking, prevent such pain and/or evil.

Because there is no other power beyond humanity except God, God must be therefore responsible, and could not be universal love? We introduced this subject in Chapter 2, but its ageless over-arching importance compels our searching more deeply.

This "problem of evil" has defied explanation by the world's greatest sages and philosophers through all human history. Unbelievers have used the inadequacies of our answers to argue against the reality of God and the usefulness of religion. One wonders how many have "given up" on God and religion because of our inability to answer this apparently insoluble problem of evil.

We proclaim that thinking of God as a separate being in heaven, who can intervene arbitrarily on Earth, actually creates this problem. Because we Christians have traditionally accepted this otherness (separateness) and omnipotence of God, good and evil could flow only from God's intervention or permission. Accordingly, the problem of evil has never been solved by even the wisest among us.

We assert, however, that Jesus, the "bumpkin" from the hills of Galilee, who embraced the inseparable unity of God in created beings, has solved this problem. Tragically, because so few explore seriously the values and priorities of his soul, few are even aware of his solution. Consequently, there is universal failure to recognize his magnificent achievement. He solved the problem of evil through his teaching, and especially his life, and death.

However, as seen already, we must insist with him that God is not external to us. Rather, God is one with the crucified Jesus, the stillborn child, the grieving parents, she/he dying with cancer, or the abandoned mother struggling alone to raise three children. God is relational love in every created being, and therefore, resides at the foundational core of joy, tragedy and every cosmic and Earthen experience.

As humans, we cannot choose all our experiences, but we can choose to love more deeply and divinely because of them, especially the pain-filled events. Therein, we express powerfully from our depths the Trinitarian love for which we are made. The disasters we endure, often demand profound faith and courage that otherwise we would never have the opportunity to embrace. Simply stated, these painful encounters force us "to stretch" our faith and love.

By overcoming such desperations, we nurture our human heroism, and express more powerfully the core of Trinitarian love within us. This expression, and nothing else, measures wholly our triumph as human beings, and our drawing closer to our beloved God. Therefore, every experience becomes for us an opportunity to love: to prove our "divine upbringing", and grow into a human success story. You and I will be eternal winners if, like Jesus, we seek to use our "calvaric" crosses as opportunities to love to the fullest.

In my previous book, *Miracles, Messages and Metaphors*, your author wrote,

> *Jesus' pain and ours provides him and each of us the chance to prove that our love is indestructible [also known as daily resurrection] ... As for God's part, she/he wills for us only the very best. And the very best for us means our participation in love [with divine, cosmic, and human dimensions] ... Nothing else has*

value except insofar as it serves in some way the heart of the divine.[7]

Evil becomes therefore our "golden opportunity" to become like Jesus, one who will give "his/her all" for our sisters and brothers. Such a lover becomes a winner, a hero, a Christ. Nothing else matters in this world of human-divine love. "What does it profit a man to gain the whole world and forfeit his life?" (Mark 8:36) Jesus destroys thereby the fear of evil and elevates our courageous virtue to divine heights. This solution of Christ proves most challenging, but if one seeks true greatness, he/she answers the challenge and embraces this solution.

Accordingly, I pledge to you my reader, "I love you." I might not physically know you, and certainly my love for you, a stranger, would differ from that of my wife and children. However, like God,

---

[7] Norman Carroll, *Miracles, Messages and Metaphors, Unlocking the Wisdom of the Bible* (Austin, TX: Synergy Books, 2010), 217-218.

love forms ideally, the root of our every relationship. The manner in which Christ calls us to express our love is <u>our decision,</u> but, as noted, its expression must arise always from a human-divine core of love. Einstein said it well,

> *A human being is part of the whole called by us universe, a part limited in time and space. He experiences himself, his thoughts and feeling as some things separated from the rest, a kind of optical (delusion) illusion of his consciousness. This illusion is a kind of prison for us, restricting us to our personal desires and to affection for only the few persons nearest us. Our task must be to free ourselves from this prison by widening our circle of compassion to embrace all living creatures and the whole of nature in its beauty.*[8]

The heart of Jesus knew no restraints in his love for God in all creation. Jesus lived and died as a man totally free to love to the fullest especially in times of trial. And so, despite his murder by capital punishment, Jesus continued to love even his torturers. He epitomizes whole human success.

Ideal human love pictures Jesus suspended on a cross. His arms extend horizontally to include all of us of every part (nationality, race, gender. religion, sexual preference, or any other part) of every whole even so-called 'enemies.' His body reaches vertically to the heights and depths from the tiniest even to include the whole Cosmos. This scene provides a life-paradigm for each of us to live in this fullness of supreme universal love: like Jesus, with person and body open appropriately to all.

Could the reason for our failure to accept Jesus' solution to the problem of evil (total love as the supreme inclusive human-divine value

---

[8] Albert Einstein, *Information Technology and Moral Philosophy* (NY: Cambridge University Press, 2009), 62.

and all that serves it) be that we don't truly acknowledge, understand, and accept God as exploding love in our own apparent tragedies; thus, we do not respond in love. We live with other priorities such as protecting ourselves and our own material values. We follow standards such as wealth, religion, education, status, health, and others. This applies to our societal as well as our individual lives. Could all human life be summarized as our journey from self to love motivation?

Our failure to prioritize God's love for each of us marks the most basic reason for our blindness. Jesus explains: *"If you were blind, you would not be guilty, but since you say, 'we can see', your guilt remains.'"* (John 9:41) Who of us "sees" in her/his depths that the God of this entire exploding, incredible Cosmos of 14 billion years is falling in love more and more avidly with insignificant me?

This divine love could be the greatest example of evolution in our Cosmos. Love is the origin as well as the product of evolution as Peck writes,

> *The process of extending oneself is an evolutionary process. When one has successfully extended one's limits, one has then grown into a larger state of being. Thus, the act of loving is an act of self-evolution even when the purpose of the act is someone else's growth. It is toward reaching for evolution that we evolve.* [9]

Our refusal to manifest our God's presiding and evolving in us defines sin as we know it. This failure thereby obstructs the evolving wholeness for which we were created. Indeed, all we are and do, finds its ultimate meaning in not deterring or ignoring, but promoting oneness in unconditional love of God, Cosmos, and humanity, the ultimate whole.

---

[9] Scott Peck, *Road Less Travelled*, 82.

One outstanding example of such promotion is our human knowledge. Quoting Zachary Hayes, Delio remarks, "Knowledge renders one, more part of the cosmic whole when it is deepened by love. It [knowledge] is never an end in itself, but always a step toward ever deeper richer love and transforming union."[10] For example, the more I come to understand your pains, joys, and dreams, the more I can appreciate and love your goodness and compassion. Knowing without loving becomes simply mere information. Knowledge like all creation serves and co-creates love, and if it doesn't, it loses its primary value.

Some experience love as boring, static, and submissive. However, the opposite is true: it's an amazing adventure of the heart and mind. Delio writes, "Love does strange things. It does not function logically or systematically; it is often spontaneous, creative, and provocative,"[11] as in you the reader and I, the author, being in a loving spiritual relationship without ever having physically met.

This spontaneity results from your love and mine calling us, at times, not to be reasonable, but to be impassioned beyond the absent physicality of our relationship. Our love has conquered time and space, and participates in eternal divine love.

I recall an experience of mine years ago. My friend, Frank, twenty-eight years of age, was engaged to Susan, a beautiful young woman, spiritually and physically. One week after their wedding, she suffered a horrendous auto accident in which she lost her right arm, and leg, and was terribly disfigured. Foolishly, I asked Frank what he planned to do. Annoyed, he replied with conviction, *"Why would you even ask? I shall care for her my whole life! I love her!"* And that is what he is doing.

---

[10] Delio, *Unbearable Wholeness of Being*, 141.

[11] Delio, *Unbearable Wholeness of Being*, 196.

Yes, the fervor of genuine love proves more compassionate and committed than mere rationality. Delio writes, "*Love [the summit of all relationships] is the essential structure of all reality, the metaphysical basis of all that exists, the eternal pattern of the universe.*"[12] Some walk, breathe, and live unknowingly in a whole world of evolving love. A trinity of explosive love loves us into existence, supports us from within a world of evolving challenge, and unites us with foundational eternal embrace.

This love (in which we participate) leads to an ever-progressing unity of all that is: Cosmos, humanity, and divinity not merely as separate objects joining together, but as divine love constituting and overcoming all obstructions. Such love is constantly expressing itself clearly and increasingly with one voice teeming in countless dialects from every distinct created being and experience.

This breathes of unlimited expansive possibilities, and gives us who are privileged to be included, cause to wonder exceedingly at the incredible mystery of this divine love in which we are invited to participate. If not careful, one could become lost in love, and become another Jesus.

However, many churches justify themselves by identifying their progress with the cause of defending the kingdom of God. Many forget, however, their founder, Jesus, did not defend himself or God's "kindom." (Matt. 26:52). He simply loved fully and appropriately, and no threat, rejection, or pain could diminish his love. If our churches are to promote God's kindom, and thrive as servant leaders, they must live more wholly the loving life of Jesus their founder.

His example applies to individuals and certainly communities as well. A recent example of such occurred throughout the visit of

---

[12] Delio, *Christ in Evolution*, 120.

Pope Francis to the United States September 24- 27, 2015. He never mentioned doctrine, law, or defense of the church, but did project a Christly image that attracted all.

Because some Christian churches devalue human love, especially sexual love, we need to remember that all forms of genuine human love manifest divine love. McBrien distinguishes four types of love in Greek. "First, *epithemia,* which is desire including sexual love; second, *eros,* the drive of union with others which brings self-fulfillment; third, *philia,* affectionate love as among brothers, sisters and friends, lastly, *agape,* total dedication to the other regardless of the personal cost." [13].

One can be tempted to restrict God's love to agape as if God dwelt only therein, but God resides within, and throughout all four types of human love; for example, genuine appropriate sexual love (*epithemia*) can ideally express the other three types. Insofar as that love is based on integrity, truth, and compassion, God becomes truly incarnate in love's growing expression. The pulsation of love vibrating through our beings measures our birthing of God and our wholeness (holiness).

Gandhi exclaimed, "I will love the next person I meet," no matter who she/he is. God is constantly inviting us to be driven by his/her spirit of love from within. Luke describes this: "Suddenly there came from heaven [the inner taproot of each] a sound as of a violent wind which filled the entire house [person or community]." (Acts 2: 2) From God in the heaven of your heart, streams a continuing passionate impulse of human-divine love seeking to consume your whole being and function and to empower with love, you and whomever and whatever you experience.

---

[13] McBrien, *Catholicism,* 976.

What if life were ninety years of loving! Possessions, dreams, health: all individuating marks including finally our whole Earthly life itself dissipated in varying spasms of time and degree. What if our only enduring preserve was the love we live throughout our lifespan! What if we discovered that in all manners of strivings only our love survived! What then?

Love becomes then not only our origin, but also our model, constant companion, and singular ultimate avenue and constituent of our divine destiny. We would understand then the epitaph on the memorial in Algeria of Albert Camus, the famed moralist and political theorist, "*Now I understand what they call glory: the right to love without limits.*"

PRAYER

Grace-filled love, we understand you are not only emotional and intellectual but ultimately decisive. Spirit of God, we are deciding this moment to live your life of love and compassion. We are aware that our love must assume different contours in our various relationships, but your love shall be our springboard, our way, and our identity. You are calling me to love you in all your beloved; therefore, I commit myself to cherishing our beloved more deeply moment to moment. As Jesus renamed Simon Peter, we accept your renaming us here and now. Love is becoming my name. Amen.

SUMMARY

Before time, divine love exploded in bestowing itself, and the Big Bang was born of God. Thus, God appeared in the Big Bang and in all that flows from it. The entire Cosmos, Earth with its plants and animals, and all humanity reflect the Godhead, and speak from within the divine language of love.

Francis of Assisi recognized God's unity with all creation, and embraced it with appropriate reverence. Thus, our love joins the divine Tsunami internally as well as externally through all creation.

This totality of divine love also solves the problem of evil. Each occurrence, despite its *egregium*, provides opportunity for one to love more deeply, and such love determines solely and absolutely the human success story.

God calls us to love but this does not assume "blanket" servility but rather acting for the maximum good of self and the other. As such love grows, all creation becomes more unified, more intimate, more in love, more Godly.

GROUP DISCUSSION QUESTIONS

1. Because all of us derive from divine love, how can each of us be unique?

2. How are we linked to plants, animals, and objects?

3. Can you explain what Zukav means when he writes, "Love is all there is?"

4. How can our God be love when God permits such egregious evil in the world?

5. Why have we not understood Jesus' solution to the problem of evil?

6. Explain why true love is neither boring nor always submissive?

7. Why is love the most worthy of all human acts?

5

CONTINUING CREATION

When I travelled to the moon, it wasn't my proximity to that battered rock pile I remember so vividly, but rather what I saw when I looked back at my fragile home – a glistening, inviting beacon, delicate blue and white, a tiny outpost suspended in the black infinity. Earth is to be treasured and nurtured, something precious that must endure."

MICHAEL COLLINS, ASTRONAUT

"What time is it?" I ask. "It's 8:30." "Are you sure?" "Yes, I am sure! Absolutely! It's 8:30!"

The truth is that time is an arbitrary changeable calculation, not absolute; for example, the annual change from standard to daylight saving time every spring and its reversal in autumn. Actually, if we suspended our measurement of time, the Cosmos would still continue.

And what about space? We look on space as emptiness in which stars and planets balance in static suspension. However, space is not empty and definitely not static. We observe the night sky with perhaps two hundred stars and planets against a vast empty unchanging blackness. That blackness, however, is burgeoning with unseen stars and planets so that, if visible, the whole sky would not be black but ablaze with light from trillions and trillions of celestial bodies of immeasurable density, without visible limit, and all in constant movement. Could this incredible vastness and dynamic symbolize the enormity of divine love that seeks to continue creating from within each of us?

Most of us would assert that. if there is anything I own autonomously, it's my life. After all, Aquinas defines life as "*sui motio*" (self-movement), and I surely possess that ability. Physicists affirm, however, that all created beings "live", in a real sense, because of the sub-atomic particles and waves of every being that swirl endlessly. We humans have merely a different form of life (reflective) than other living beings.

Space, time, and life represent three ways of measuring one massive evolving reality. Delio writes, "*We can no longer divide up life, space, and time into self-isolated fragments. Rather, reality is a single, organic, evolutionary flowing.*"[1] These three become mere markers as rocks or reeds in a cascading stream of tsunamic divine love from within and through the whole Cosmos

A theology professor shared with me years ago that spirit could not mutate downward into matter; nor could matter mutate upward into spirit. However, we now know spirit and matter are different forms of energy, and are therefore interchangeable. One is not inferior to the other. All is love; all is flow; all is reflecting the "divine".

Denis Edwards paints the same picture but from God's viewpoint,

> *The story of the universe and of life on Earth and everything that science can tell us about its evolutionary history, is part of a*

---

[1] Delio, *Unbearable Wholeness of Being*, 176.

larger story, the story of divine self-bestowal ... [and] exists within the larger vision of the divine purpose to give God's self to us.[2]

Again, consider a brook bubbling along its way. It becomes deeper and shallower; it turns right and left. Rocks and banks change its course. All these represent passing moments we call incarnation, creation, living, dying and rising. The spring water represents God's love always flowing, always supporting, through the vagaries of the eternal course.

Jesus spoke of life, but referred consistently to all life (physical and spiritual) as meaning the movement of the whole person toward or away from the author and sustainer of life. Unlike Jesus, we attend chiefly to the parts, and fail to see that our lives, like all created reality, are constantly journeying as a whole from love to love, in God.

---

[2] Denis Edwards, "Teilhards's Vision as Agenda for Rahner's Christlogy, ed. Ilia Delio, , *From Teilhard To Omega, Co-Creating An Unfinished Universe* (Maryknoll, NY: Orbis Books, 2014), 59.

Were there space and time before creation? Certainly not! They are a part and a measure of this continuing creation. Was there God before creation? Yes, but God in process of self-effusive and diffusive love, resulting in tiny quanta, massive swirling planets and stars, and even our consciousness, all of which are moving and evolving. Therefore, we may describe creation as the ongoing exploding detonation of divine love filling every nook and cranny, including you and me.

When reflecting on creation, believers tend to think of one moment when God created from nothing. However, we have already considered creation not as an isolated act but a continuing process of loving. Panikkar explains:

> *Creation does not happen in time [one moment in time], but brought about time along with it. Creation is not a temporal event ... It has nothing to do with any "Big Bang" at the beginning of time. Creation is the continuous becoming of the creature [beyond all human timely measurement]. In such a perspective, if God created once, he has to 'go on' creating constantly, [we cannot measure divine activity by time, a human construct]. Creation is neither a temporal act nor a gigantic work of an all-powerful Engineer. Creation is the constant becoming of being.*[3]

Creation is the ongoing sign of irrepressible spiritual energy of love, the unfinished symphony of divine love, and we join God as his Beethovens.

Genesis does not state that God created from nothing; in fact, Genesis 1:1 states that God actually brings order from chaos. The biblical footnote presents an alternative translation of Genesis 1: 1. "God began creating heaven and Earth, the Earth being then a formless void

---

[3] Panikkar, *Rhythm of Being*, 98-99.

with darkness over the deep, and a divine wind sweeping over the waters."[4]

Creation can only derive from three possibilities:

1. *An exclusively physical action of some description* – perhaps, a physical chancy Big Bang without reasonable origin, order, motivation, consistency, God, or soul. It just happened! This denies what is plainly visible to an "objective eye" that observes order, purpose, wholeness, and consistency within us and all about us.

2. *The traditional objective static God who decides to create.* This is the whimsical childhood God of Eden to which many still cling. This God has few answers to today's questions as proposed by reason and science. It even dares to question adult searching itself. Could this clinging to a childhood God by so many adults, even some hierarchs, be the root reason so many are rejecting religion in these days of scientific maturing? Ursula King quotes Teilhard's Divine Milieu: "Is the world not in the process of becoming more vast, more close, more dazzling? ... Will it not burst our religion asunder? Eclipse our God?"[5]

   We assert that will not happen, for God could not be static, not if God is love. God, as we perceive him/her, is also evolving, and will not be superseded. Our mission is to shout that dynamic message of these pages from the rooftops, for God, according to Jesus, is truly and purely love. Jesus is sending you and me as today's apostles with that precise message!

3. *This is God embodying all creation to which we have been referring.* The Big Bang is the new genesis: the new story that ac-

---

[4] *The New Jerusalem Bible* (NY: Doubleday, 1985), 17.

[5] Ursula King, *Spirit of Fire: The Life and Vision of Teilhard de Chardin* (Maryknoll, New York: Orbis Books, 1996), 38.

cepts and rejoices in the findings of scientific truth, while discovering ever more deeply the impact of divine love as seen in creation's ongoing evolutionary progression. John Haught explains:

> *The emergence of the first instance of life can be thought of as welling up from the Earth's and the universe's own bountiful potential of Cosmos. It is more appropriate to conceive of God as the ultimate depth and ground of nature's resourcefulness than as a magical intruder.*[6]

Thich Nhat Hanh reinforces clearly this fundamental truth by referring to Paul Tillich: "Tillich has said that speaking of God as a person is just a figure of speech. He said that God is the ground of being. This makes me think of the water that is the ground of being for the wave."[7]

---

[6] John F. Haught, *Responses to 101 Questions on God and Evolution* (New York: Paulist Press, 2001), 23.

[7] Thich Nhat Hanh: *Living Buddha, Living Christ* (New York: Riverhead Books, 2007), 154.

This notion of creation raises again the question of Adam and Eve: not the story of our mythic ancestors, but their meaning. So we ask: Did Adam and Eve ever actually live? Our response: "Of course"! They live today! Every human being has Adam and Eve in her/his heart. These two represent the self-centered part of our ego. Yes, Adam and Eve are alive and well as part of every one of us still struggling with God's inner call to wholeness in us as we continue our journey through and to the real Eden.

We acknowledge God as the ultimate foundational lover in union with this created magnificent panoply. We insist on the fullness of that love in every created being, and this is why creation seethes with divine dignity.

Many believe God created gratuitously: that is, God exercised, at a point in time, his/her option to create. This view has attraction because it seems to reveal God as one who, from free choice, loved by deciding to create, and therefore we owe God total gratitude. However, Delio points out,

> *For Teilhard, the relationality of God's triune nature makes creation more than an act willed out of intellect or desire; creation is the truly beloved [extension] of God, and hence fulfills God's desire for [mutual] relationship.*[8]

God still merits our complete gratitude – not, however with created being as a passive, inferior, separate being, but as a relational partner. God can't be a fixed being existing to create arbitrarily, for that eliminates God's full presence in relationships, and adds an unwanted imperial and inappropriate dimension to his/her presence.

Because God is love, God must create, and that creating is not from nothing. For then, the created would necessarily be separate from

---

[8] Delio, *Emergent Christ*, 47.

the creator. Rather, the creating Spirit bursts from the spiritual into the physical because divine love is boundless. This divine imprint present in the Big Bang extends through all its progeny making us, therefore, all children of God in and through the Big Bang. God is as present in you and me as in the Big Bang. God is love flowing through all created beings fully and forever.

Therefore, even the term "presence of God" lacks the unimaginable intimacy of God's oneness with us. What a shame that I, we, do not appreciate our being created extensions of divine love. Thus, in reality, our God is seeking from within the entire beloved creation, an ever deeper and more expressive partnership of creating, saving, and inspiring. All human history, including what is described in the Bible, may be summarized in one phrase by Abraham Heschel, "God, in search of man"[9]; but let's not forget that God is not only the searcher but also the searching and the searchee.

Delio remarks, "Creation, in a sense, complements God not by supplying something God lacks, but by relating to what God is as divine love."[10] Thus, our gratitude is not to a God of objective otherness; rather it's to God in all of reality including ourselves. We see, hear, smell, taste and touch the presence of the Trinitarian Godness in all the created, from the before moment to the now moment, from love to love in this continuous, astonishing, evolutionary process. Thanks be to God for God!

This Cosmos, Earth, and all creation are "shot through" by and with God's Spirit, the Spirit of explosive and all-inclusive love. Our privilege is to recognize, embrace, and live this Trinitarian Spirit of love by walking in this moment with the heart and in the sandals of Jesus of Nazareth who lived fully in God's Spirit-filled humanity.

---

[9] Heschel, *God in Search of Man*, 136.

[10] Delio, *Emergent Christ*, 47.

Because all creation is in change (evolution), God who stands in relationship to evolutionary change, must also therefore be changing, (evolving). Silence to those who still cling to a static perception of God, for how could God not be present in the process of evolution itself in all its parts? Delio writes:

> *Teilhard realized that the Greek metaphysical structure supporting Christian doctrine was too static for the dynamic world of evolution as science describes it, The notion of God in the midst of the cosmogenic [cosmic evolutionary] process provides a metaphysical basis to the concept of emergence in nature.*[11]

Because our God of love and truth lives in every creature, whether cosmic or Earthen, O'Murchu adds, "*We detect its power in the inspired, creative energy that we name as the Originating and Sustaining Mystery, otherwise called, the life-force, or God.*"[12]

Some years ago, I climbed a portion of Mt. Rainer. I stopped on one particular crest to observe the sweep of snowy white and pine green cascading thousands of feet below. The awe-filled changing beauty, life, and mystery overwhelmed me so that I was forced to wonder at the Spirit breathing not on but in these slopes.

Many of us can gaze at a marvelous sunset or lake, and attribute such beauty to God. This is truly a gift, but there is more to the scene than merely reflecting on God's beauty. Every created being from the heights of cosmic experience to the unknown of human hearts, manifests God's actual dwelling therein, and becomes God's love partner in surpassing unity.

---

[11] Delio, *Emergent Christ*, 4.

[12] Diarmuid O'Murchu, *Evolutionary Faith, Rediscovering in Our Great Story* (Maryknoll, New York,: Orbis Books, 2002), 202-203.

The theologian Leonardo Boff draws the consequence, "All things in nature are citizens, have rights, and deserve respect and reverence."[13] The same holds true in my and your daily experiences and encounters. God does not work on us like a controlling puppeteer (as a Geppetto) pulling the strings of our limbs (as a Pinocchio). Rather, God works in us and through us as our intimate lover with as much oneness as we allow.

We reside in a world of divinity in and through materiality existing before our very eyes, of which many of us remain sadly unaware. Delio joins many Christian authors who refer to creation as the first book of revelation. It's true! God reveals him/herself in the wisdom, beauty, and community (*koinonia*) of created munificent magnificence!

Thomas Berry proclaims:

> *It is clear that the universe as such is the primary religious reality, the primary sacred community, the primary revelation of the divine, the primary subject of incarnation, the primary unit of*

---

[13] Leonardo Boff, *Cry of the Earth, Cry of the Poor* (Maryknoll, New York: Orbis Books, 1997), 133.

redemption, the primary reference in any discussion of reality or of value,.[14]

In the same manner, Gerard Manley Hopkins observes ecstatically: "The world is charged with the grandeur of God."[15]

Each created holon could not possibly portray the excelling benevolence of God, but each does express authentically, if only partially, God's brilliance. Hence, many eco-theologians refer to creation as the body of God. Indeed, one could refer to divine expression rather than divine creation.

Why, I wonder, do we not hear mention of this cathedral of creation more frequently in church homilies and gatherings, when God is summoning us to an omni-lateral love affair with all our created brothers and sisters. In a word, God is loving all created beings into existence, and calling us moment by moment to plunge more and more fully into his/her loving depths.

We have noted that creation is an ongoing flooding of divine love from the core of all that is. This continuing emergence relates all beings and events to each other. This is visible especially in creation and incarnation. Delio attributes the following to Rahner: "Creation and incarnation are not two separate events of God; rather, two moments, and two phases of the one process of God's self-giving and self-expression."[16] Actually, all persons and events reflect this ongoing divine emergence, but these two stand as preeminent exhibits of this overflow of divine love.

---

[14] Berry, *Teilhard in 21st Century*, 25.

[15] Gerard Manley Hopkins, "God's Grandeur," *The Top Five Hundred Poems* (New York: Columbia University Press, 1992), 792.

[16] Delio, *Emergent Christ*, 153.

Remember the analogy of our brook. The tulips of Spring, the death of a beloved, the first cry of a newborn, and all experience signal in some unique way God's new creation and incarnation. Every moment breathes of divinity's continuing overflow and inflow of love through all creation. Teilhard writes, "By the virtue of the creation and, still more of the incarnation, nothing here below is profane for those ... who know how to see."[17] I would suggest that creation and incarnation are mutually and equally reciprocal.

We all exist as numberless partial luminaries of God's enlightening. This is not to suggest that there are greater and lesser intensities of such divine brilliance, but it does point to our uneven acceptance of love's challenges pursuant to our specific nature. We remember love always preserves freedom. God, love, is still creating and still assuming multiparous cosmic and Earthen existence in us and through us.

There is more good news. Teilhard writes: "*In action, I adhere to the creative power of God; I coincide with it; I become not only its instrument, but its living extension.*"[18] Chardin is identifying himself and us with God in expressive creation. Therefore, each of us is co-creating, co-saving, and co-inspiring with our God. Delio explains further by referring to the work of Zachary Hayes, the Franciscan theologian:

> *While it might seem fantastic that we are co-creators in the universe, the meaning of being the image of God [Gen. 1:27] refers to the capacity to give birth to God in [ourselves and] creation, that is, to [express] God in our lives. Bonaventure's understanding of the human person is one of co-creation in Christ.*[19]

---

[17] Teilhard de Chardin, *The Divine Milieu* (London: Collins & Sons: 1960), 66.
[18] Teilhard, *Divine Milieu*, 62.
[19] Delio, *Christ in Evolution*, 139.

Once we understand that creation is a continuous emergent process of birthing, we can accept that God and we remain pregnant with new forms, new beings, and new beauty. As one example among countless: is not our sexual, conceptual, and natal process in forming new human splendor, symbolic of our cooperating with God?

Likewise, what of those who labor daily in blistering heat to pick our fruits and vegetables? Others teach our children for paltry wages. Many abandoned parents must work, and then worry over their children who return from school to an empty apartment. What of our sanitation workers, and they who can't find work?

All these folks, and I am sure you also, are contributing in a unique way to the amelioration of creation. What new marvels, often ignored, have God and you created today?

We concluded Chapter one with words from Etty Hillesum, the young saintly Jewess who was gassed to death in Auschwitz. We return to her once more, and complete this chapter on creation with her following oracle of prophetic wisdom:

> *One day we shall be building a whole new world. Against every new outrage and every fresh horror, we shall put up one more piece of love and goodness, drawing strength from within ourselves ... I [shall listen] to myself, allow myself to be led not by anything but what wells up from deep within.*[20]

For us, that day has arrived; God will live forever as an exemplar in Etty's heart. She, a great co-creator, summons us to the same, not from the fossilized ovens of Auschwitz, but from the heart of their conqueror: evolving love.

---

[20] Etty Hillesum, *An Interrupted Life, The Diaries of Etty Hillesum* (NY: Pantheon Books, 1981),198.

PRAYER

Dearest Etty: How profoundly we admire in awe your faith and love as you wait with your sisters and brothers within the death camp. Help us to realize, through our decision, that your beloved God of life and love
resides also within us so that we might spill our "spiritual blood" for our sisters and brothers. Help us to co-create with our God a world of greater reverence, compassion, and beauty with the love of the \Holy Spirit as it reigns gloriously in your life to and through its eternal course.
Amen.

SUMMARY

We tend to think of God as creating us from nothing, and then sustaining us. This relegates God as separate from us, capricious, and temporal. God, however, is separate from nothing, for then whatever is separate is, to that degree, beyond God's purview. Not possible! Further, God is not deciding whether to continue supporting us or not, but is so compelled. Finally, God is not subject to human measurement of time or space. Rather, before time, God, of and from himself, overflows into creation, and thus eliminates all possibility of caprice.

God in us is creating by fulfilling, beautifying, and sanctifying. God thus elevates us to co-creator and co-incarnator. To in-carnate is for God to assume flesh; to create is for God to generate. One might argue that incarnation is a form of creation, but, in the end, they are one and the same. How supremely gifted we areto be God's consequence and residence!

GROUP DISCUSSION QUESTIONS

1. How are space, time, and life related to the Big Bang?

2. Why the importance of God compelled by love to create rather than choosing to create?

3. How does the myth of Eve and Adam initiate our own person life-journey?

4. We tend to consider creation as God fashioning the original being from nothing at one moment. How is this faulty reasoning?

5. Many theologians assert that created beings represent the "body" of God. What is their reasoning?

6. How can we explain creation as an on-going event?

7. Why can we affirm that you and I are co-creating with God?

6

UNIVERSAL EVOLUTION

*Evolution is not something that simply applies to life on Earth;
it applies to the whole universe.*

JOHN POLKINGHORNE

Recently, while sitting in my backyard, in a kind of pensive mood engendered perhaps by reading Tennyson, I happened upon this perceptive line from his Locksley Hall: "*Let the great world spin forever down the ringing grooves of change.*" Putting the book down, I gazed at the overarching blue, and noted a few cumuli floating lazily across its expanse. A breeze rose to turn the pages of my book, and fluttered the leaves of a nearby oak causing a bird to take flight, and a squirrel to flee. "My God, Tennyson is right! Everything's in motion. My blood is pulsing; my thoughts flee one before the other. I've been constantly aging for too many years, and, despite my supposed stillness, every part of me is moving."

Come to think of it, physicists, as noted in Chapter 5, tell us the physical is composed of atomic and sub-atomic particles, and everything at this level is in motion. That means everything is changing – including you, me, and all that is. Because that is true, God is also changing, for God is in relationship to us, and when a part of the relationship changes, the whole relationship changes. My safe comfort zone of apparent divine stability is suddenly shaking. After all, culture and church has always taught me there is one truth on which I can fully depend: God is unchanging.

It's no wonder my security is becoming insecure. I recall the story of the sailing schooner docked securely in its home port. Word arrives that this vessel must depart immediately for distant seas of unknown depths and threatening weather; it's now burdened with the uncertainty of the worrisome journey of changing and becoming.

Becoming suggests however positive change of which evolution is a prime example. Evolution applies to the becoming of new species; for example, the human species of today relative to its precedent animal species of 500,000 years ago. We cannot arbitrarily erect walls of limitation to the on-going powerful process of evolution that has been overcoming stasis for nearly 14 billion years.

We have all raised anchor on our own journey, and are even now sailing in uncharted seas. Indeed, the revolving Earth itself and the entire Cosmos are changing, becoming. There is no static homeport for us or any created being except in our innate evolving. Teilhard adds pointedly: "Nothing can any longer find place in our [mental] constructions which do not first satisfy the conditions of a universe in process of transformation."[1] Could this represent the ultimate necessity for faith?

Teilhard adds, as noted, "Evolution is a process of becoming."[2] Evolution, however, is more than growth, for it includes growth into another species. When such journeying leads to growth from another species, we call it evolution. For anyone to deny the presence of evolution is not myopic; it's total blindness. One would be forced to say: no new species ever formed from the original. Butterflies do not spring from caterpillars, and God who is Spirit never created matter.

Thomas Berry, famed eco-theologian, unpacks this understanding of evolving reality into five orderly dimensions.

1. The universe and everything in it results from a series of irreversible ongoing advancements begun, as far as we know, 13.7 billion years ago called the Big Bang.

2. This evolutionary process includes the psychic and spiritual as well as the physical. Thus, when an individual or community (for example, a church or government) fails to progress, it loses touch with the evolving march of all remaining creation, and forms a widening anachronistic chasm of irrelevance with cur-

---

[1] Teilhard de Chardin, *Christianity and Evolution* (New York: Harcourt Brace, J. Jovanovich 1971), 78

[2] Diarmuid O'Murchu, *Our World In Transition* (New York: Crossroad Publishing, 2000), 127.

rent culture. Might this explain the failing state of church today?

3. Earth enjoys, according to our current knowledge, a unique privileged status with life, intellection and all cosmic components bonded in certain communion. This flows from the web of the whole we discussed in Chapter 1.

4. Teilhard observes, "*Man is a cosmic phenomenon, not primarily an aesthetic, moral, or religious one.*"[3] This demands from us a cosmic shift in priorities from self to self as part of the whole, and corresponds with that Christian model of journeying from priority of self to the priority of the cosmic Christ (cf. Chapter 7).

5. Our human component assumes therefore the role of lover and caregiver not exploiter of this divine marvel called Earth. As we discussed in Chapter 5, we humans must refuse to tolerate the continuing exploitation of Earthen wholeness. Moreover, as human, as Christian, as part of the ultimate whole, and as co-creators, our solemn duty is to nurture nature as God-inspired, and God-expressed throughout. Consider deeply in your heart: am I as a Christian, and is my Christian community leading in fulfilling today that role?

From Bede, Delio summarizes the stages of evolution: "The evolution of the universe is from [spirit to] matter to life to consciousness in the human, and from human consciousness to divine life and consciousness."[4] Surely, this ageless and all-comprehensive growth ought to be of prime interest to any church that seeks to lead its followers to its fulfillment in Christ, the Omega Point. However, have you heard even one homily, or attended any church sponsored

---

[3] Teilhard de Chardin, *Letters From My Friend*, ed. Pierre Leroy (New York: Paulist Press, 1976), 137.

[4] Delio, *Christ in Evolution*, 118-119.

learning session on this critical subject? Oh churches! Lead us beyond dogmatism to inquiry, dialogue, resolution and love.

Introducing evolution brings immediately to mind the person and name, Charles Darwin. Darwin (1809-1882) was an English geologist whose views on evolution have caused his being listed among the most influential humans of all time. His discovery encompasses two simple propositions:

> *First, all forms of life descend by way of gradual modification over the course of time from a common ancestor; second, the explanation of this gradual modification arises from natural selection, [meaning] those organisms most able to adapt to their environment, survive ... and produce offspring.*[5]

Critics such as the zoologist Jean Grasse, paleontologists Stephen Gould, and Niles Eldridge, and others critique varied dimensions of Darwinism, but these fundamental propositions endure. For example, each human body contains about 60 trillion cellular parts, and each grows and sustains as an ear, eye, skin, etc. They then somehow, all relate necessarily and orderly to sustain the whole: you and me. And consider that every cell in the universe relates with countless electrochemical responses moment to moment.

Christians, truly all of us, can accept these truths without fear. Indeed, we are mightily grateful for this comprehensive divine orderly plan. The philosopher Patrick Byrne clarifies six succeeding progressive stages of this evolutionary plan:

1. **Cosmogenesis.** This refers from the orderly evolution of the universe to the emergence of the planet Earth with diverse centered circulations; e.g., electrons surrounding nuclei, planets around stars, stars in galaxies, etc.

---

[5] Haught, *Responses*, 7.

2. ***Geogenesis.*** This refers to the evolution of Earth about 4 billion years ago, probably from a fragment of the sun which, with chemical elements from stars, crystallized into rich mineral deposits to form the spherical layers of Earth.

3. ***Biogenesis.*** This birth of first cellular life forms about 3.8 billion years ago from a welling up from the Earth's and universe's bountiful potential.

4. ***Psychogenesis.*** Some scientists would say life has neither purpose nor direction. Teilhard de Chardin argues that increasing complexity (for example, the onset, and development of consciousness) proves psychic purpose.

5. ***Anthropogenesis.*** This is humanity's developing power to reflect upon itself as an object and a center of experience and reactions thereto.

6. ***Christogenesis.*** This speaks to the birth of recognition of our activities as contributing to an evolving wholeness. The maximum wholeness of truth and love of which person and society are capable, is the Omega Point, the Risen Christ.[6]

Unfortunately, most of us have been taught, and have never questioned the immutability of God. We have accepted that all is changing except God. We could always depend on our solid static God who forms a kind of comfort zone. However, as noted prior, we must admit that we ourselves are evolving, and so God who is love embraces us as we are now, which differs from what we were moments ago. Therefore, God's embrace of this moment has changed or evolved from God's embrace of previous moments. Delio adds,

---

[6] Patrick Byrne, "The Integral Visions of Teilhard and Lonergan," in Ilia Delio, Ed., *From Teilhard to Omega* (Maryknoll, New York: Orbis Books, 2014), 85.

> *If we are to be faithful to the integral relationship between God and creation, then we must admit that if the Cosmos is in evolution, then God is in evolution as well ... God is not static immutable being but dynamic relational love. God is eternal, all-embracing fields of love, holons within holons, persons within persons.*[7]

Panikkar points out, "If the conception of the world has changed so radically in our time, then there is little wonder that the ancient notions of God do not appear convincing."[8] How sad that we must admit to the shrinkage of religion. Religion has retreated from exploring this challenging universal *koinonia* (communion) of the whole cosmic community, and often promotes instead, a divisive, exclusive, power-driven, and self-serving salvation.

Because we no longer believe with the authors of Genesis in a flat Earth beneath a blue dome, we also discredit a bearded elderly male holding court atop that dome as a sky-God. Certainly, a central task of informed Christians is to help introduce church to its great friend and provider: evolution.

Delio quotes Nicolai Berdyaev, the Russian philosopher;

> *People are afraid to ascribe movement to God because movement indicates the lack of something....But, it may equally be said that immobility is an imperfection, for it implies the lack of the dynamic quality of life.*[9]

She adds, "The evolution of God is the God of ever newness in love."[10] Delio carries us even one-step beyond to say that, "Because

---

[7] Delio, *Emergent Christ*, 104.

[8] Panikkar, *Rhythm of Being*, 186.

[9] Delio, *Emergent Christ*, 3.

[10] Delio, *Emergent Christ*, 7.

creation is essentially related to God, who is love, [so] evolution is the unfolding process of God in love."[11] Love, God, becomes, therefore, the driving force of evolution. God is also goodness and truth, and all of us seek these (albeit often strangely), inch-by-inch, generation-by-generation. God's creation is deliberately moving and evolving therefore toward the summit of these, the Omega Point, the Risen Christ.

We must not fall into the trap of considering the Omega Point as only an external goal of humanity in the future. The Omega Point, the cosmic Christ, lives today in our individual and communal spirit as the evolving summit of love, truth, and goodness to which we consciously and subconsciously aspire. This point becomes our energizer, path, and goal: in a word, Our Savior. Teilhard agrees: "I believe that the messiah whom we await ... is the universal Christ, that is to say, the Christ of evolution."[12]

---

[11] Delio, *Emergent Christ*, 37.

[12] Teilhard de Chardin, *Christianity and Evolution*, 205.

Thus, evolution becomes an enduring, deepening, broadening rush of love, slowly but surely attracting by its very nature each of us and the created whole. Delio refers to Teilhard's use of the term "amorization" (from the Latin word *amor*, meaning "love":) to describe "*the process of unfolding love in evolution.*"[13]

In other words, Teilhard views both communal and individual humanity advancing as God's enticement from love to love. Teilhard likens this amorization to a group of miners trapped by accident deep underground. They yearn, plan, and work without ceasing for light and air.[14] So, evolution thirsts desperately in all creatures for truth, love and goodness.

This journey in love is savaged along the way by ignorance, malice, injustice, misunderstanding, and sin, but the evolutionary process justifies our indomitable, and undying hope. Our role, individually and communally, is to overcome these obstructions, and promote this precious procession toward the Omega Point of love and truth.

Despite the onslaught of iniquities and inequities, a careful review of centuries and millennia does reveal slow labored progress; for example, education of peoples, improving status of women, minorities, and gays, resistance to slavery, and the grudging surrender of religious and political tyranny.

Jesus largely ignores personal salvation, and yet, so many who claim to be his disciples, define Christianity in terms of personal salvation. Many even assert the date of their being saved. Rather, his message calls us to love God, neighbor and all creation, and then trust God for our destiny. "Father, into your hands I commend my spirit." (Luke 23:46) Bede Griffiths elaborates on God's complete commitment to his whole family: "Behind all the conflict and confu-

---

[13] Delio, *The Unbearable Wholeness of Being,* 99.

[14] Teilhard de Chardin, *Christianity and Evolution,* 205.

sion is this hidden mystery of love that is behind the whole universe."[15]

Just imagine you and I, as disciples of Jesus, living today for the prime purpose of loving as he loved. What an Eden he and we would co-create! Without political intent, but with our love-vocation in mind, one embraces words by former Senator Ted Kennedy, "The work goes on, the cause endures, the hope still lives, and the dream shall never die."[16]

About this evolutionary progression of 13.7 billion years and counting, Delio writes:

> Is not blind, random, or meaningless change. Rather, there is a unifying influence in the whole evolutionary process ... that continues to hold the process together and move it forward toward greater complexity and unity.[17]

She continues by telling us that influence resides within reality as "*Tendency, desire and purpose.*"[18] These entice us to journey forward on the path toward truth, goodness, and love which we by nature desire. Remembering these are of God, we come to understand that they become the divine lure which attracts us. This is why movement and growth pervade the whole universe including Earth and all its sojourners; why we seek what we seek.

This indomitable searching, this "fire in the belly,"[19] takes different forms in all created beings. Among humans, despite our ignorance

---

[15] Bede Griffiths, *The New Creation in Christ* (Springfield, Illinois: Templegate Publishers, 1999), 104.

[16] Edward Kennedy, *True Compass A Memoir* (NY: Hatchette Book Group, 2009), 542.

[17] Delio, *Emergent Christ*, 89.

[18] Delio, *Emergent Christ*, 89.

[19] Sam Keen, *Fire in the Belly* (New York: Bantam Books, 1991).

and waywardness, this fire continues to burn progressively in all of us as our inherent search for truth and love. Jesus exclaimed, "I have come to bring fire to the Earth and how I wish it were blazing already." (Luke 12:49)

We may analogize the cascade of divine love as a pre-cosmic volcano erupting in the fiery lava of love extending into all depths of beings through all times even to us today. This conflagration of love has a human voice.

> *Deep within his conscience, man discovers a law which he has not laid upon himself ... Its voice ever calling him to love and to do what is good ... His conscience is man's most secret core and his sanctuary. There he is alone with God whose voice echoes in his depths.*[20]

One might ask why it is that love, and not obedience, intellection, or principle surges through the whole Cosmos and its parts. We respond: because God is love and God presides through all. Thus, evolution consists really of God (love) "unfolding" and manifesting her/himself in union with the beloved Cosmos and humanity ever more deeply and universally through her/his wondrous creation.

We are privileged to be caught up in this intoxicating process of love that is beyond all comprehension. This love compels God to become one of us, and is called incarnation which surely continues in all of us. Each of us, of both genders and all ages, cultures, and religions, assumes thereafter the motherly role of receiving divine inspiration and birthing once again the living emerging Christ in unique form.

Could this ongoing incarnation, which is really the daily painful growth of Christ individually and communally, represent also the

---

[20] *The Catechism of the Catholic Church* (New York: Paulist Press, 1994) No. 1776.

second coming of Christ? Could incarnation and the second coming describe two markers in the ongoing universal stream of amorization?

This procession of love surely draws all of us together as lovers, insofar as we choose to participate in this human-divine trysting. O'Murchu declares that as this marvelous process continues, so also does its complexity. He adds, "Prior to the existence of all life forms, very simple single-celled creatures inhabited our world. Life-forms became progressively more complex, more elegant, and more mysterious in nature."[21] This complexity does not however, mean more complicated. "It is about life becoming capable of mutual enrichment through diversity and variety."[22]

Thankfully, modern science is rediscovering the breadth and depth of richness in this concept; meanwhile, traditional religion continues to have fear and suspicion of this awesome complexity. John Haught points out that the cosmic theology we are discussing herein, rests on the emerging of divine love seeking new paths of expression now and in the future, new dawns of dialogue and trust.

We must not become like the foolish virgins of Matthew 25 who are ill prepared, and finally fall dead asleep. We are the "People of God" who search for the rising rays of the new dawn, and revel in Christ's glorious emerging.

Religion, awake! Our presence looks to the future for new light not the darkness of the past![23]

Delio, with deference to Teilhard, breaks down the complexity of evolution:

---

[21] Diarmuid O'Murchu, *Our World in Transition* (New York: Crossroad, 1992), 126.

[22] O'Murchu, *World in Transition*, 126.

[23] John Haught, *Deeper Than Darwin* (Boulder, Colorado: Westview Press, 2003), 172.

- *Organization.* Evolution follows an axis of ever-increasing organization. Consider for example, the organizing concurrent from the Big Bang to this moment. "The cell gropes [see chapter 9] or feels beyond itself [in love] for what it can use; indeed, the whole of life is groping ... Teilhard's word 'groping' acknowledges a dependence on chance, but it also affirms that life has a direction, an orientation, a preference ... it prefers increased life."[24] One outstanding example is the development of conscious thinking and functioning in daily life with clear and reasoned motivation.

- *Convergence.* This organizing or groping is *convergent*. Because all consciousness seeks truth and love, it emerges deliberately toward a point of evolving supremacy of truth and love, Teilhard's Omega Point. Even the malevolent criminal commits his/her crime for what he/she believes is true and good. Because all conscious beings act by nature for what they believe is true and good, all are deliberately converging toward what is supremely true and good.

- *Omega Point.* Because supreme truth and love represent the pinnacle of human achievement and because Teilhard was preeminently Christian, he called the Omega Point of creation, the Risen Christ, which we have previously noted, and will explore in Chapter seven.

Death remains for us the ultimate moment of Earthly evolution – when we shed our shadows, and dismantle our masks. The author, Andrew Marvell, writes that life is but an introduction to death, and death, to departure. It is true that most fears denote the dimension of departure. The poet speaks sadly of it this way:

---

[24]Delio, *Christ in Evolution*, 69.

> *Thy beauty shall no more be found,*
> *nor in thy marble vault shall sound*
> *my echoing song; then worms shall try*
> *that long preserved virginity, and your*
> *quaint honor turn to dust and into ashes*
>
> *all my lust. The grave is a fine and private*
> *place, but none, I think, do there embrace.*[25]

Rare the person who does not succumb to doldrums of sad spirit when reflecting on death. Marvel dwells on death's finality, and its loneliness: that's what hurts. In my senior years, I can witness to this fear and the apparent unknown as challenging. Despite how it may appear, death signals only our Earthen transcendence. We continue our evolving as privileged spiritual beings with the God of love as our guide within the same whole of reality.

Christ suspended on the cross above Earth remains our great teacher and life preserver. His lesson proclaims that despite whatever terror, events, including death, can inflict, our love overcomes and transcends insofar as it replicates his love. We call this triumph of love, resurrection. The crucified Christ pictures the summit of love's victory over pain and death. Death could not diminish his love one iota, and hopefully not yours, for love safeguards us through death unto life. Indeed, love destroys death.

Like Jesus, we must first climb our mountain of life to reach its peak. Therefore, our lifelong climb is an evolving movement toward that peak, the summit of love. As we climb, our vision converges on the summit, but the summit is not the goal; rather, t'is the figure who hangs above the mountaintop: the Christ.

---

[25] Andrew Marvel, "To His Coy Mistress", *The Top 500 Poems*, ed. by William Harmon (New York: Columbia University Press, 1992), 230.

He, the full reflection of glorious love, beckons us to continue our climb to its triumph: the Promised Land, the Omega Point, the Christ rising in us.

PRAYER

Lord God, truly we are called to see your presence in all creation. But, we also fix our vision on the goal, your son, who reigns as the cosmic Christ at the hilly summit of all creation, the summit of human divine love. We resolve to follow him up our Calvary to embrace you in all our brothers and sisters. We pledge to strive ever forward on that way to you, the pinnacle of truth and love, the evolving Omega Point of all blessed evolution. Thank you for your glorious gift of evolution: the journey of Cosmos, Earth, and humanity to your summit of love.
Amen.

SUMMARY

We have noted previously that all is changing, but strictly speaking, when that change results in a new species, we call it evolution. In general, however, evolution remains a very gradual emergence of new forms. There have been six progressions of evolution: Cosmos, Earth, life, psyche, humanity, and Christocentrism. These encompass all creation. We have learned well the old story of God reigning from heaven; now we realize God is the power of love surging through all these universal facets.

We might ask why love and not another power? Our answer: because God is love. The march of love continues because of the lure of truth and love which draws us indefatigably toward its fulfillment, the Omega Point, the Risen Christ. This applies even among those who are not conscious of their own seeking. Thank God, truth and love (God) lure all of us within and toward the divine.

GROUP DISCUSSION QUESTIONS

1. If evolution requires change in species, how does the presence of humanity demonstrate the truth of evolution?

2. Explain the six progressive stages of evolution.

3. How can one demonstrate the order and direction of evolution?

4. What is the Omega Point?

5. Evolution is related in essence to the universal pervasion of love. Explain that relationship.

6. Evolution has two central characteristics: organization and convergence. Explain and distinguish these.

7. Why can we state that Christ's crucifixion really portrays the ultimate victory of love?

7

THE CHRIST OF THE COSMOS

The spiritual thirst of Christ is a love-longing that will last always until we are altogether whole in him.

JULIAN OF NORWICH

Christians! Who is your savior? Is it Jesus Christ? Not exactly; not if you believe in the man born in Bethlehem, and raised in Nazareth who died on a cross. That person was named Jesus, Luke 1:32.

His name is not Christ. That's his title, function, or career, and it means "savior." In his era, "*Some people were eventually given a second name to express what the person had really begun to mean to others. So, Jesus came to be called Christ, meaning the anointed one, the Messiah, the savior.*"[1] That's what we, his followers, mean by calling Jesus, the Christ. In this sense, Moses, Mohammed, and others (including ourselves) may be revered as "christs" by their sisters and brothers.

---

[1] Edward Schillebeeckx, *Interim Report on the Books Jesus and Christ* (New York: Crossroad Publishing, 1982), 21.

We Christians have, however, concentrated on the historical Jesus as well we should, but Delio quotes Panikkar who digs deeper: "Jesus is Christ, but Christ cannot be identified completely with Jesus. Christ infinitely surpasses Jesus."[2] Jesus remains for us Christians the one historical person who alone has accepted fully the Christ, the Spirit of God on Earth, the Spirit of truth and love. As a result, Jesus never sinned, and therefore never lied. Even he recognized, and proclaimed, "an any of you convict me of sin? If I speak the truth, why do you not believe me?" (John 8: 45-46)   Why do we also refuse?

More positively speaking, the gospels proclaim his love excelling in all circumstances. Having thus accepted the Spirit of Love fully, we have faith that Jesus is divine, the ultimate presence of our God of love on Earth. This is why we pray in liturgy, the Greater Doxology: "Through Him (Jesus the Christ), and with Him, and in Him, in the unity of the Holy Spirit, all honor and glory to you, almighty Father, forever and ever."

As we have pointed out, viewing God in the heavens manipulating his creatures down below on Earth as an omnipotent beneficent autocrat utterly misses the mark. Rather, consider God pervading every shred of creation, as we saw in Chapter 3; God: self-diffusive, loving, and identifying with every holon, including every cell throughout the whole creation.

The name of God in this relationship is Christ. Christ then is God relating to creation in love. So, Christianity is not fundamentally about penance, sacrifice, or obedience to Church (though these can play an important role), but about promoting unrestrained, evolving love: Christ.

---

[2] Delio, *Christ in Evolution*, 89.

Evolution is not our enemy; it's our foundation, our motivation, energy, and goal. Denying the truth of evolution is denying our assuming a new divine species: that of Christ. Incarnation is a two-way street: God assuming flesh so flesh can assume divinity, and both through evolution.

As noted, Jesus presents that one human person who has received and lived God's Spirit completely. Delio explains, "Divine love explodes in the person of Jesus in an explicit way [fully and clearly] so that he is recognized as the Christ, the cosmic person, the paradigm of relationality."[3]

Thus, Jesus becomes the greater Big Bang, for Jesus mirrored fully God as human. This ignites for us new dreams, new life, new victory over violence and death, new wholeness, and a new people. Therefore, Jesus the Christ calls each of us to become not Jesus, but Christ, cosmic people, models of Christic transparency. To study, explore, and evolve into Christ as did Jesus, becomes our primary career in life, but sadly, few ever bother to know Jesus on a meaningful human level, and thus abort their Christic career.

I recall as a boy dreaming of a career like my hero, Red Barber. Red (Walter O'Neil) was a radio broadcaster for the Brooklyn Dodgers baseball team in the 1940s. I dreamt of traveling with Red and the team and describing the action. Perhaps, you had a hero whom you wished to imitate. Today, all of us, whatever our religion or lack thereof, have the same hero, Christ.

You might now be saying, "That's crazy! I don't even believe in Christ." To which I respond: "Christ is the archetype (the ideal universal example) of every human heart, representing yours and humanity's highest aspirations."[4] Why? Because, as noted earlier, eve-

---

[3] Delio, *Unbearable Wholeness of Being*, 122.

[4] Miguel Serrano, *C.G. Jung, and Hermann Heiser: A Record of Two Friendships* (New

ry human by nature seeks truth and love, and Christ alone of all people has, as we have seen, fully lived through Jesus such a human life. Therefore, Jesus could exclaim, "I am the way, the truth and the life." (John 14:6) For anyone to deny Christ, therefore, is to deny her or his own humanity seeking truth and love.

This same divine fullness of truth and love dwells in us, and speaks to us through our true and growing conscience. Christ thereby calls each of us from our core to be a Christ in our own corner of the world, travelling the road to complete fulfillment according to our capacity for truth and love.

Jesus is the supreme lover – he realized the summit of what humanity and creation can be and can do, and therefore, he presents the full human presence of God on Earth. "Christ symbolizes the personal center of love that bursts forth in Jesus, and empowers our own lives to converge in love. Christ represents the capacity to live in love and hence in God," proclaims Delio.[5]

There is even more to Christ. As we have seen, Christ, as the divine font and exemplar of truth and love, lives in every one of us. Therefore, Christ abides in you insofar as you accept truth and love; and, as such, Christ yearns to express and even to embrace through you each created being you touch. There is no person, nor being, nor event in our universe (save sin) that Christ refuses to support through you.

In other words, our loving relationships spring from Christ, our divine lover, who pervades our entire being and all others. Christ seeks from the core of and throughout our person to express himself in a way bespeaking that divine love, which Jesus expressed fully. Our privilege is to concretize uniquely Christ in our lives.

York: Schocken Books, 1965), 56.

[5] Delio, *Unbearable Wholeness of Being*, 105.

Disastrously, many Christians today deny or fail to understand this truth, this cornerstone of Christianity. They center their religious experience on following laws, rituals, and/or doctrines to which Jesus, rarely if ever, referred, or to defending an institution, which Jesus never knew, and would largely have reformed if he had known its course.

We have written of the Christ resident within all created beings, but we must remember John 1:1-10: "In the beginning was the Word and the Word was with God and the Word was God ... He (the Word) was in the world that had come into being through him." The Word is God's self-expression known in relation to created being as Christ. Christ may then be said to be God known through and in all created beings. Because Jesus accepted the Spirit of God with his entire being and in all his relationships, he is God's presence on Earth: the fullness of the Christ. Therefore, the Word is incarnate wholly in Jesus and partially in all remaining humanity.

This is the cosmic Christ who thus divinizes material creation in the sense that Christ is pervasive love therein. We can touch Christ, God, solely through this glorious creation. This Christly unifying of God and creation gives our material world its supreme dignity and value. This explains why Jesus *exclaims*: "I have come not to judge the world, but to save the world." (John 12:47)

Delio exclaims,

> *When the adjective 'cosmic' is used to describe Christ, it means that Christ is the instrument in God's creative activity, the source and goal of all things, the bond and sustaining power of the whole creation, the head and ruler of the universe. Basically, the term relates Christ to the entire [whole] created order, emphasizing that*

Christ's relationship to creation extends beyond the compass of Earthly humans, and includes the whole Cosmos.[6]

Therefore, in Christ, divinity, Cosmos, and humanity embrace as one enduring all-inclusive love-affair. Truly, Christ is becoming incarnate continuously throughout the universe in every created being: each of which manifests divinity in a new unique way from moment to moment. Mary, the mother of Jesus speaks for every created being when she exclaims, "My soul proclaims the greatness of the Lord." (Luke 1:46)

---

[6] Delio, *Christ in Evolution*, 50.

Jesus becomes our savior not by satisfying what some wrongly consider his Father's grotesque demands of a bloody atonement for sin, but rather by loving to the fullest and giving us such saving example by which we can live the life of God on Earth. It is Christ through Jesus and all creation who summons us through every age to join him in a dynamic ecstatic love affair with God in all creation.

Our degree of acceptance and embrace of this God-given privilege of love measures our response to that command of Jesus, "Come, follow me", and also our degree of salvation.

Thus, penance, prayer, attending church services, and following church rules carry value only insofar as they help us to live this life of reckless abandonment to Christly love. Merton writes, "Whatever I may have written, I think, can be reduced, in the end to this one root truth: that God calls human persons to union to himself [love] and with one another in Christ."[7]

Nearly every one of us thinks, walks, and talks in some way with self-defense and/or self-empowerment as our primary motivation. Self is the primary name of our game. Jesus insists that the work of our whole human life, patterned on his example, is to transform self-motivation into Christ motivation.

Our life-standard thus becomes: "What's best for Christ, not me." This is not to deny love of self, but to assert that love of Christ includes and transcends love of self. This is why we do not proclaim "Jesuanity" but Christianity. Christ seeks to heal today our blindness so that we can see the astounding greatness to which he calls us.

---

[7] Thomas Merton, quoted in *The Thomas Merton Studies Center*, Nov. 10, 1963 (Santa Barbara: Unicorn Press, 1971), 146.

Such love, such goodness, compels me to live for the Christ in me and you, and you, for the Christ in you and me. This ultimate radical revolution has a name: Christianity. Imagine one man and his disciples trying to transform human nature itself, to establish a new way of living, a new people, a new world order. Talk about revolution! And we with Christ are the revolutionaries!

Therefore, this momentous truth: Christ is reaching out through me, you and every created being to support us and every other being in an all-inclusive never-ending whole love affair. You, I, and all are rooted in Christ, divine love. This is why we need, seek, and give love even as we do physical food. We know food is the fundamental need of all physical life; without it, we perish.

Likewise, love is the fundamental food of all spiritual life. Without it you and I die spiritually. Thus, if I love no one, and no one loves me, I am spiritually dead: I live in hell. Opposed to spiritual death, however, is our living love-embrace of all creation as Christification: that is, Christing all God's creation and ourselves by realizing and living God's dwelling within. Thus, we do not have to wait for death to enter heaven.

This depicts our life-journey, our evolution in Christ. Meister Eckhart speaks of God's chief aim as giving birth – that is, God's entering ourselves with his/her entire divinity, and begetting sons and daughters in us. God enters wholly the ground of our being.

For us privileged humans, Delio describes this Christification as including a coming to explicit consciousness. We must not construe this as a mere intellectual experience, but that of the whole person deciding and promoting the explosive tsunami of divine love springing from our human depths and pervading everything in sight.

To illustrate, in classical dance, the two partners seek to achieve a certain unity. This unity symbolizes the "Christifying" dance of self and reality, and reflects harmonious symmetry (despite an occasional discordance of step). Still, the overriding thrust of this eternal dance is ever evolving toward the ideal dance: from Christ to Christ, the Omega Point. Teilhard points out, "I believe that the Messiah ... whom we all without any doubt await, is the universal Christ; that is to say, the Christ of evolution."[8]

We have traveled far beyond a one-sided emphasis on sin, guilt, orthodoxy, and private salvation that describe much of today's religiosity. Those churches that cling to that outdated story are not keeping pace with the divinely inspired scientific and cultural changes occurring so swiftly, and are "paying the price" in reduced members, acceptance, and credibility.

Many in church leadership tolerate these smaller numbers; for example, Pope Emeritus Benedict XVI stated that the church must accept lesser numbers and stature. That signals, however, a loss of the church's opportunity to reach those of contemporary vision, a failing in its essential evangelistic mission, which indeed church is now experiencing.

Delio writes, "Love is the [radical and] essential structure of reality ... Christ is the center of all reality because Christ is the fullness of love, that love which is the most complete integration and union of divinity and humanity."[9] To understand Christ, we must explore the life of Jesus who was fully Christ. This demands our deliberately searching out Jesus, especially his motivations, priorities, lifestyle, and how he, alone of all humans, radiates whole love even amidst egregious personal agony.

---

[8] Teilhard de Chardin, *Christianity in Evolution*, 95.

[9] Delio, *Christ in Evolution*, 120.

Such exploring of Jesus becomes the supreme work of our lives. Sadly, however, where are they who are willing to spend the time or effort? I am reminded of the words of the poet, Ron Seitz in his Song for Nobody: "Can you think of a greater tragedy or worse loss or sin than our not understanding the real message and person of Jesus?"[10]

I remember clearly, my approaching the parking lot of a large church in Oaklawn, Illinois at which I was presenting an adult formation retreat on the person of Jesus. I was delighted to see the lot packed with cars. But, when I entered the church, there were only fourteen people present in a congregation of 1300 families. Sadly, I learned a huge crowd of hundreds was attending a basketball game in the church gym next door. I understood.

"As he drew near and came in sight of the city he shed tears over it, and said, 'If you too had only recognized on this day the way to peace! But in fact it is hidden from your eyes.'" (Luke 19:41) If God's love overflowed fully, and was fully accepted in the Big Bang, then the whole reception of God's Spirit by Jesus can be called the new Big Bang, and incredibly, Christ calls each of us to be a new Big Bang, a new people, a new Christ.[11]

We have distinguished between the Jesus of history and the Risen Christ, the Spirit of God overcoming, through persistent God-given evolution, our own and society's apathy, violence, and self-indulgence. New divine birthing is occurring in every created being; therefore, as we have seen, every moment becomes incarnational. Amazingly, God is asking us to become what God is: creative, saving, and inspiring. Yes, each of us dons an ever-new bril-

---

[10] Ron Seitz, *Song for Nobody: A Memory of Thomas Merton* (Ligouri, Missouri: Liguori Publications, 1995)

[11] Delio, *Making All Things New*, 76.

liance insofar as Christ is able to live through us, and we, through him.

He stretches his arms to exclude none, and include all in his embrace: the nearly fourteen billion year old Cosmos, our exploding galaxies, our Earthen beauty, and all humanity. Instead of excluding anyone, Jesus commands us to treasure every thing and everyone. "Go to the open roads and the hedgerows and press people to come in, to make sure my house is full!" (Luke 14:23) No judgments! No requirements! No guilt!

Jesus teaches us to intensify and multiply divine birthing in ourselves and throughout creation by loving unconditionally as he did. This represents the second coming of Christ occurring even now in the continuing growth of Christ in each of us. This will initiate a mighty tidal wave, a tsunami of compassion and love growing and evolving until it breaks on the shore consuming all creation. Its presence in us ignites the fire of God to burn away injustice, apathy, and evil, and to promote the prophetic words of Teilhard de Chardin.

> *The day will come when, after harnessing the air, the winds, the tides, and gravity, we shall harness for God the energies of love, and on that day, for the second time in the history of the world, human beings will have discovered fire.*[12]

So, I make the words of Paul, my own: "Maranatha; the grace of the Lord Jesus Christ be with you. My love is with you all in Christ Jesus." (1 Corinthians 16:22b-24.

---

[12] Teilhard de Chardin, *Toward the Future* (Boston: Mariner Books, 1975), 86.

PRAYER

Great cosmic Christ, you are the foundation, the bonding, and goal of all that is. Though we on our own are unworthy even to be, still we reach out from our insignificance to promise you that we will try to wipe away your tears and ours by consecrating our lives to you this moment. I will live primarily not for possessions nor personal gain, nor competitive edge but for your cause, your kindom. Compassion, non-violence, and reverence will become the hallmark of my daily living. These will draw me day by day to you, my Omega Point, the Risen Christ, my destiny in love now and forever.
Amen.

SUMMARY

My name is Norman Carroll, but Jesus Christ is not the name of our savior. Rather, it's Jesus of Nazareth. Christ is his title; what he was called to be, the fullness of truth and love. Like Jesus, God calls us to be a Christ. We can't achieve that fullness, but we can seek to live it every day in every circumstance. This marks the supreme human journey: to transform from self-motivation to Christic passion. Do I write, do you work, do we relate to others firstly to use them in achieving fame, power, or money, or to manifest goodness, honesty, and compassion?

God is calling each of us from our core to augment the tsunamic love coursing through creation. This is God's work, and the more we participate, the more Christly we become.

GROUP DISCUSSION QUESTIONS

1. In what sense does Christ surpass Jesus?
2. How can we view Jesus and ourselves as the greater Big Bang?
3. If one does not believe in Christ, can he/she still aspire to be a Christ?
4. What does the "cosmic Christ" mean?
5. In what way was Jesus the most radical revolutionary in all human history?
6. If God can only give her/himself fully, why does each of us vary in lifestyle?
7. When is the second coming, and what does it look like?

8

CHURCH IN CRISIS

"It is religion itself, more than any other cultural force, which has undermined and damaged the universal conviction of God's unconditional love. And in this process formal religion frequently robs people of ... how the divine works in our midst ... Yes, religion has achieved a great deal, but ... [it] tends to create codependency rather than the liberation and empowerment
that all the great scriptures claim to deliver."

DIARMUID O'MURCHU

Too many years ago, Joan, my wife, and I brought our newly born to St. Anthony's Church in Fort Lauderdale, Florida for baptism. We had asked our favorite priest to celebrate the ritual, and for good reason. Father was friendly, a fine preacher, and well respected throughout the community. Nevertheless, later, Father "turned out" to be a brutal child molester. The bishop then transferred him to several other parishes. Eventually, this charade was discovered, and he sits today in a prison cell dreaming of his return to ministry.

I still marvel in disbelief, as much at his desperate cry for power as at the fact that church could aid and abet such atrocity at those about whom its founder exclaimed, "Anyone who is the downfall of one of these little ones who has faith in me would be better drowned in the depths of the sea with a great millstone around his neck." (Matthew 18:6)

This sexual-abuse scandal within the church does not stand as an isolated event. Too many clerics have been involved, too many hearts have been broken, and too much credibility has been destroyed. The foundation of these scandalous relationships proves the pathology of the patriarchal control system that church hierarchy still promotes to this day. Bishop Geoffrey Robinson writes, "All sexual abuse is first and foremost an abuse of power ... in a sexual form."[1] Oakley and Russett state further,

> *The 'acknowledged gravity' of the sexual abuse crisis itself and its mishandling by so many bishops at home and abroad is ... grounded in, builds upon, reflects, and certainly discloses long established pathologies in the clerical culture in our modern structure of ecclesi-astical governance and in the well-entrenched and almost instinctive mode of ecclesiological thinking prevalent among so many of our church leaders.*[2]

Fear of bishops and/or superiors paralyzes and infantilizes too many clerics, who then seek power in aberrant and abhorrent behavior. Control generates fear of the controller. Many "Fr. Smiths"[3] will compose their homilies this week, consciously or subconscious-

---

[1] Geoffrey Robinson, *Confronting Power and Sex in the Catholic Church* (Collegeville, Minnesota: Liturgical Press, 2007), 12.

[2] Francis Oakley and Bruce Russett, *Governance, Accountability, and the Future of the Catholic Church* (New York: Continuum International Publishing Group, 2004), 9.

[3] "Smiths" is used here as a fictitious name, and with apologies to any actual priests who carry that name.

ly, with fear of offending church hierarchy or doctrine, instead of that searing passion to lead the community to Christ. This is why we rarely if ever hear relevant homilies on the sexual abuse scandal, family planning, the gay experience, ecumenism, women's equality, pastoral concern for divorced persons, the merciful humanity of Jesus, participatory church governance, the tragic closing of parishes and schools, etc. – issues of these of such great interest to the baptized laity.

In that same vein, I recall a vicar of my diocese bemoaning to me, *"It's a shame that, when we summon the ordained to the chancery, they come in fear."* Sadly, he was correct. Delio remarks

> *"The Catholic Church is losing members as it becomes increasingly irrelevant to a world in need ... It seems the church is slowly collapsing from within. It is a progressive diminishment, a grasping for air ... Instead of evolving, it is devolving – its very presence is thinning out to the extent that in some areas of the world, such as parts of Western Europe, it is dissolving into history."*[4]

Pope Francis understands the underpinnings of such declining interest in church, "Christian theology is not a closed system incapa-

---

[4] Delio, *The Emergent Christ*, 115.

ble of generating questions, doubts, interrogatives - but is alive, unsettled and enlivened. It has a face that is not rigid; it has a body that moves and grows; it has a soft flesh. It is called Jesus Christ."[5] Jesus did not threaten anyone, but welcomed all (women, non-followers, gays, the uninformed, lepers, and sinners) with open arms, warm heart, and the admonition to sin no more. I agree enthusiastically with the courageous Episcopal bishop John Shelby Spong, whom O'Murchu quotes:

> *"I anticipate that most of what we call religion today will die in the next century. Rigor mortis has already set in. Out of that death, however, will come a new beginning. I am glad that I have lived to see the birth pangs."*[6]

A disillusioned priest asked me recently whether I thought church would survive current hierarchical controlling behavior. Let's be very clear on this subject: church will survive for two excellent reasons.

- First, Jesus initiated a new movement, and, despite its continuing dalliance with power, his Spirit in community will endure. Crucifixion was not a one-time event. It does and will continue, but the same can be said of resurrection. As tragic as crucifixion might be, more glorious will be resurrection.

- Second, we humans are as much societal as individual. Therefore, Jesus, in his wisdom, eschewed a one-man effort, and instead called others to stand with him. Togetherness lies at the heart of religion and even Godhead. Religion will survive, but, as always, with evolving forms.

---

[5] Joshua J. McElwee, "Catholicism can and must change, Francis forcefully tells Italian church gathering," *National Catholic Reporter*, Nov. 10, 2015,

[6] Diarmiud O'Murchu, *Adult Faith* (Maryknoll, New York: Orbis Books 2010),181.

A central reason for the tenacious absolutism of some churches is the regal image of God that church hierarchy has proposed, but which no longer works. Panikkar writes, "God is always God for a world, and if the conception of the world has changed so radically in our times, there is little wonder that the ancient notions of God do not appear convincing."[7]

Despite lip service to God being love, many church leaders have by their own behavior and teaching convinced the baptized that God reigns as a remote taskmaster who judges us daily, and and who will finally dispatch us to heaven or hell. Such church leaders have perpetuated the idea that God is judging us from "up there." This promotes a passive supplicant church membership. By contrast, Delio proclaims wisely:

> "God is not the divine mechanic above but the power of love within – the unbearable wholeness of love pushing through the limits of being to become more visible and alive. God beyond us, within us, and around us, must return to the center of what we

---

[7] Panikkar, *Rhythm of Being*, 186.

are if we are to evolve toward a new ultra-humanity....God cannot do for us what we must do for ourselves."[8]

Most Christians identify church with God's "kindom," as if church were the whole and not a part. Therefore, they reason that, by defending church, they are defending God's kindom. Actually, "church," which word Jesus uses just three times, represents not the kindom but a way to God's kindom, which word Jesus uses 165 times. By claiming to be the kingdom, church is thwarting God's whole kindom of love. which is non-visible. "The coming of the [kindom] of God does not admit of observation and there will be no one to say, "Look! It is here! Look, it is there!" For look, the kindom of God is among you." (Luke 17:21)

In the introduction, we quoted Thomas Berry saying that we are in-between stories, and indeed we are. But should not church leaders be leading us critically in search of the new story as it appears in these pages and elsewhere? Most importantly, Jesus, as founder, has commissioned his disciples to free humanity in an indefatigable search for truth and love.

By still promoting God as an external judgmental entity, many denominations seek implicitly to claim God for themselves, or assert that, "We are more favored by God than you." Cannato quotes Denis Edwards: "So much harm has occurred as religious factions fight over the question about who has the "real" God. The answer? We all do. God is not defined by religion, only human beings are."[9] As we have seen, religion's role is to lead us to Christ, and not redirect the journey to itself.

---

[8] Delio, *Unbearable Wholeness of Being*, 207.

[9] Judy Cannato, *Radical Amazement*, quoted Denis Edwards (Notre Dame, IN: Sorin Books 2006),151.

Mary Evelyn Tucker and John Grim write in the introduction to Thomas Berry's *The Christian Future and the Fate of Earth*:

> *He [Berry] opened up a gateway for Christians to reform their tradition by making an Exodus passage into the modern world. He called for a transition like the first Exodus experience of the Jews out of Egypt, a passage into modernity, something church has so often resisted.*[10]

Culture is forcing church leaders to make a pivotal decision: either abandon their insular attitude toward people, science, and postmodernity, or engage them in courageous dialogue. "I have come not to condemn the world, but to save the world." (John 12:47)

We Christians must understand that religion is but one function of culture which is changing rapidly and radically. The more culture changes, the more church seems to resist that change. So, the chasm between culture and church continues to widen. Paul Crowley exclaims,

> *If theology cannot engage the sciences, then it has no voice at the table concerning the significant issues facing humanity today, [and] risks self-marginalization. Christian faith itself is at risk of seeming irrelevant, and God increasingly distant from the horizon of human understanding.*[11]

It's not that church must follow culture, but it surely ought to follow its founder whom it claims to worship. Christ has something to say to culture and science, but let's be honest! Most current church governance too often does not reflect the compassionate Christ, and is impairing his work of universal whole-making. However, the worst

---

[10] Thomas Berry, *The Christian Future and the Fate of Earth* (Maryknoll, NY: Orbis Books 2009), xvi.

[11] Delio, *The Unbearable Wholeness of Being*, quoted Paul Crowley, 152

dynamic of contemporary church remains the apparent lethargic ignorance of this crisis by most church people both clerical and lay. For them, it's "business as usual." Yet for Jesus, this is the hour of crisis!

> Then he came back to his disciples [in Gethsemani], and said to them, "You can sleep on now and take your rest, [but] look, the hour has come when the son of man is to be betrayed into the hands of sinners. Get up! Look, my betrayer is not far away!" (Luke 26:45-46)

Blasé Paschal, French philosopher, suggested this pivotal question, "Are we in our own Gethsemane sleep?" Could we even now be sleeping with Peter, James, and John? Review even summarily the culture we now experience, and one must agree that Christianity has fallen into deep sleep. Delio observes,

> If we are to draw a connection between the word catholic and the mission of Jesus, we would have to rely on its root meaning, 'according to the whole,' for what Jesus preached was not a church defending itself in the face of opposition but the in-breaking of the reign of God.[12]

Can you imagine Jesus protecting, at all costs, himself and his doctrines by condemning or excluding those who question honestly? Jesus did not guard himself, and surely condemned no one while insisting on the values of whole truth and full love.

This reminds me of a story told by the renowned journalist Bill Moyers of Joseph Campbell, who was attending in Japan a conference on religion. Campbell overheard an American delegate saying to a Shinto priest, "We've been now to a good many ceremonies, and have seen quite a few of your shrines, but I don't get your ideology.

---

[12] Delio, *The Emergent Christ*, 62

I don't get your theology." The Japanese paused as though in deep thought then slowly shook his head. "We don't have theology ... We don't have theology. We [just] dance."[13]

Scripture scholar Steven Doyle declares that to believe that any person or thing (even church) other than Christ can save is to believe in idols. The success of church is measured not by the beauty of its buildings, nor the numbers of attendees, nor the dollars in the collection baskets, nor its doctrinal decrees, but by how profoundly and powerfully it draws us to Christ in each other.

C.S. Lewis writes, "The church exists for no other purpose but to draw people into Christ ... If it is not doing that, all the cathedrals, clergy, missions, sermons, even the Bible itself, are simply a waste of time."[14] Further, church will succeed only insofar as it replicates Christ who attracted thousands of people not because of his wealth or imperium (of which he had none), but by his compassion and commitment.

Apropos of this, Rev. Martin Luther King wrote on April 16, 1963 the following from the Birmingham City Jail:

> *The judgment of God is upon the Church as never before. If today's church does not recapture the sacrificial [nature] of the early church, it will lose its authenticity, forfeit the loyalty of millions and be dismissed as an irrelevant social club.*[15]

Do you ever wonder how so much of today's church could be so closed, when its founder was so open, embracing, and compassion-

---

[13] Joseph Campbell, *The Power Myth* (NY: Doubleday, 1988), xix.

[14] C.S. Lewis, *Mere Christianity*, (New York: Simon and Schuster Touchstone 1996), 171.

[15] Herb Frazier, Bernard Edward Powers, Marjorie Wentworth, *We Are Charleston Tragedy and Triumph at Mother Emmanuel* (Nashville, TN: W Publishing Group, 2016), 18.

ate? One questions whether the mainstream church will regain its true Christian character.

I firmly believe church will overcome the chasm between it and Christ. As in the early centuries of martyrdom, it will again look beyond itself to Christ for its ideals and energy. It will not die. Church evolves like everything else on its journey to Christ, the point of supreme attraction, the Omega Point. We are witnessing such evolving in the example of Pope Francis. No person or human system can forever, ultimately and fully resist Christ's power of truth and love which attracts humanity so passionately. This is especially true in a church, which claims Christ as its model and founder.

Church, if genuine, challenges us with the divine call to exceed the limitations of our own love. All creation bears this movement toward wholeness, which springs from the DNA of love that permeates all that exists. Love exudes from its very essence: forgiveness, healing, giving, and making whole; not dividing and condemning. So we question, "Is my church following the path of compassionate love which drove its founder to Calvary, the summit of love? Does it reflect this love in its governance, the empowering of all its members, and its avid passion to follow its founder?" In a word, we can assess the authenticity of a Christian Church by how closely it identifies with the compassion and world-view of its beloved founder.

Such a church stands starkly before us. Members of the Emanuel AME Church in Charleston, South Carolina gathered for Bible study June 17, 2015. They welcomed warmly Mr. Dylan Roof who joined them at 8:06 PM with a handgun hidden in his backpack. Mr. Roof participated, and prayed with them for about an hour, and was so moved by the talk of Christ and love he nearly forsook his plan of murder. However, finally, the crazed young man stood and began firing his death-dealing weapon. Nine disciples of Christ died in that serene sanctuary.

Roof appeared by video June 19 at his initial court hearing. Felicia Sanders, who had survived by pretending death, saw her son, Tywanza 26 throw himself before his aunt to protect her. Felicia watched them both die in this rage of red. She, with heart and soul breaking, spoke to Roof through the video,

> *We welcomed you Wednesday night in our Bible study with open arms. You have killed some of the most "beautifulest" people that I know. Every fiber in my body hurts, and I'll never be the same ... we enjoyed you, but may God have mercy on you.*[16]

---

[16] Herb Frazier, Bernard Edward Powers, Marjorie Wentworth, *We Are Charleston Tragedy and Triumph At Mother Emmanuel* (Nashville, TN:, W Publishing Group, 2016), 19..

Anthony Thompson said, "I forgive you; my family forgives you!" Ethel Lance, who lost her mother, said, "You took something very precious from me, and I will never talk to her again. I will never be able to hold her again. But I forgive you." Such heroism does not spring from lethargy or boredom but from having touched Christ, and embraced his message. Now, they walk in his sandals. This is church at its best. These folks lived and died for each other in Christ. They expressed cosmic love in Charleston. Christ calls the whole world to such community of love; we call it church.

Delio writes:

> *Christianity is a religion of [radical] evolution because it is marked by self-emptying love that gathers together and creates anew. The life of Jesus Christ anticipates a new creation whereby love of God, love of self, and love of neighbor are gathered into a new unity, a new love, and a new future ... What took place in the life of Jesus must now take place in humankind.*[17]

What then is the work of church? To serve the ultimate whole by promoting it and its parts with Christly heart and acquaint all creation with its divine origins, intimacy, destiny, and universal wholeness in God. When church fulfills this role, it becomes not merely a religious community but a whole new people dedicated to promoting the Christ in all creation. This is the true goal of evangelization: to draw people to Christ not merely to church. Christ, the revolutionary, calls us to become this new people of God, dedicated to be a kinder and more compassionate people than the world has ever witnessed, even to giving life, as he did, for the cause of love. Teilhard counseled in 1945: "The modern world is not irreligious – far from it. It is simply that the sudden injection of a massive dose of a

---

[17] Delio, *Unbearable Wholeness of Being*, 109.

new life-sap is making the religious spirit ... boil-up, and take on a new form."[18]

Jesus never dreamed of a one-man show but an evolving movement of people who would not be coerced, but rather motivated to choose truth and love with all their being. He gathered men and women of every persuasion: zealots, sinners, fishermen, doubters, Jews, and gentiles. He then challenged them to aspire to the very heights of human-divine love. He asked them to identify with him and his mission: "The Spirit of the Lord is upon me, for he has anointed me to bring the good news to the afflicted. He has sent me to proclaim liberty to captives, sight to the blind, to let the oppressed go free." Luke 4: 17-18. His work thus becomes our work: to manifest God from our depths and to fulfill in our circumstance God's cascading love through and beyond the eons of time. All who participate, comprise church. The aforementioned doctrines, rules, and organization are necessary, but always serve the lofty lessons of love, which Jesus taught us.

John Haught provides an example of the resistant pace of this Christly vision in these second axial years. "Pope Pius IX expressed in 1877 the suspicion that Darwinism is a "mask of science" behind which there lurks a purely materialistic vision of nature ... Pius XII in his encyclical *Humani Generis* (1950) granted that the human body may have evolved naturally over a period of time, but insisted that God creates each human soul directly ... [Finally], Pope John Paul II in 1996 agreed that the evidence for biological evolution is convincing."[19] However, Darwin had published his findings 137 years earlier, and science had long since given up on church's openness to scientific truth.

---

[18] Teilhard de Chardin, *Christianity and Evolution*, 174

[19] Haught, op cit., 41.

Reluctance by church to embrace and explore this new reality of scientific truth has cost it dearly in numbers and credibility. Diarmuid O'Murchu mourns this tragic failing:

> *Its numbers continue to decline with less than 50% going to church at Christmas and Easter, and less than 20% for the remainder of the year. Its influence on political, social, and scientific developments is minimal; no serious thinker today pays too much attention to church teachings. Increasing numbers of disillusioned believers seek a revitalized [sometimes bizarre] church in sects, clubs, and in a vast array of alternative spiritual movements.*[20]

Some have likened this path for institutional church as the pain of communal crucifixion, which must precede resurrection. If true, much of church must die in the manner Jesus died; that is, filled with love and compassion even for supposed enemies, and this kind of death is sadly not in evidence.

Jesus lived three qualities of servant leadership that church must adopt if it is to gain credibility, and genuinely seek wholeness. We will explore these fully in a forthcoming book, but, because of their importance, we note them here:

- *Transparency.* Any church worthy of Christ will exercise its authority "in the open." Jesus traveled and taught openly, "Jesus answered him [Caiaphas] 'I have spoken openly to the world...I have said nothing secretly'" (John 18:20). Surely, he desired his disciples to follow his lead in openness. Today's church labors with opacity. For example, why can't his baptized disciples of today participate in recommending aspirants to the diaconate and priesthood? Further, traditionally, a Vatican congregation selects bishops secretly without consulting the

---

[20] Diarmuid O'Murchu, *Our World in Transition* (NY: Crossroad Publishing 2000), 116.

local church, and then requires its acceptance. Certainly, the disciples of Christ have a right in Christian justice to participate in the selection of those servant leaders who will directly impact their lives. These servant leaders would thus be sounding a Christly tone of openness and empowerment to the "People of God". Then, the community can participate not in choosing political "ladder-climbers", but leaders who would be willing to give their lives in service.

- *Accountability.* Church servant leaders have serious responsibilities to the baptized. Still, unless there is grave scandal or upheaval, church leaders remain in authority without apparent supervision or meaningful regular review. Even corporate executives remain accountable to stockholders. Church leaders seem immune to higher authority, and the baptized who pay their salaries. This style of rule appears not participatory but monarchical. Every level of church governance should participate in checks and balances. The Second Vatican Council called it collegiality

- *Redress.* We have discussed herein love and truth as foundational to all our relationships. Surely, if Church continues to demand full internal assent to doctrines and praxis, it must, in justice, maintain an office of review, inquiry, and discussion at all levels of governance. All would enjoy access to this office with clerical and elected lay membership. Thereby, church would join in the precious human search for greater truth and love.

Religion is still well positioned, to lead this evolutionary journey to Christ, but, for it to play a leading role in whole-making, it must be willing to sacrifice its very self, and thereby gain its very self. "Then, speaking to all, he said, 'If anyone wants to be a follower of mine, let him renounce himself, and take up his cross and follow me.'" (Luke 9:23) John McKenzie asserts that "when church authority uses any other power than the power of love, it ceases to exhibit its distinctively Christian and ecclesial nature ... A display of power will usually settle matters, [but] it can and often does at the same time destroy the Christian rapport between authority and its subjects."[21] Such control has become counter-productive and self-defeating.

Church is a familial home where we learn to love wholly in all our relationships. Indeed, God intends religion and church to have servant leaders not power-figures in leading our evolution into wisdom and love. This grand evolving process constitutes the second coming of Christ, and is happening even now in many hearts and in a newly energizing open church, which is emerging from its human-divine womb. As one who has spoken in over 200 churches, I have firm trust in church rising from the ashes to give Christ's saving waters to a world parched with thirst. Indeed, church presents our soul communal hope, and it will rise, born anew in the Spirit of the Risen Christ. Thanks be to God.

PRAYER

Oh, Christ of cosmic love, present and beyond all space and time, help us to acknowledge our littleness, our insignificance on this tiny planet midst the fullness of the universe. Grant that our women and men of church, temple, and mosque may deeply grasp that they are merely avenues to your intimately loving Godhead within, so that our houses of worship may eschew all that is not of your humility and compassion. May our houses of worship evolve to reflect yourself evermore in their being through you our Lord and Savior. Amen.

---

[21] John McKenzie, *Authority in the Church* (Kansas City, Mo: Sheed and Ward 1966), 177, 179.

SUMMARY

The sexual abuse scandal within the church did not arise from a vacuum but rather from the anguished cry of some infantilized clerics. A system of authoritarian rule has robbed them of much personal solidarity: thus, their frightful search for personal empowerment. Such hierarchical control is being rejected also by contemporary culture and so we are viewing severally declining interest in church and religion

Church leaders ought to realize church exists to draw people to Christ and not itself. The more it mirrors him, the more it will succeed. However, defending his turf was not on Christ's agenda. To accomplish its goal, church governance must incorporate three essential dimensions: transparency, accountability, and redress. This demands faith in Christ and the baptized, and represents a giant step on the path to genuine ecclesial resurrection.

GROUP DISCUSSION QUESTIONS

1. Explain the true cause of the sexual abuse scandal among Christian ministers.

2. What is the future of the Christian church?

3. What distinguishes church from God's kindom?

4. What influence is church effecting on our changing culture?

5. What measures a successful church community and our choice of church membership?

6. How did members of AME Church in Charleston in South Carolina mirror a true Christian church?

7. Describe the church of today that Jesus would join?

9

DESTINED BEYOND TIME AND SPACE

*""Easter is the demonstration of God
that life is essentially spiritual and timeless."*

Charles M. Crowe

Dickens famously writes; "It was the best of times; it was the worst of times; it was the age of wisdom; it was the age of foolishness." He is referring to late 18th century Paris and London, but this also refers to every age, every city, and each of us as we struggle with the supreme paradox: life, death, and our resultant angst over both. Often, we avoid even uttering the word "death." We prefer misnomers such as "passing away" or "no longer with us." James Whitcomb Riley states poetically: "I cannot say, and I will not say that he is dead. He is just away."

The master plan of wholeness to which we have been referring, includes even death by revealing its role as the great opportunity in our evolving cosmic journey. Because it is inconceivable that the ageless, fullness of love could abandon suddenly and totally its beloved, love and life prevail through death. Haught tells us that

> *Scientists have discovered that carbon compounds, the chemical building-blocks of life, are abundant in outer space ... If the universe is so charged with potential life, then ... the emergence of the first instance of life can be thought of as welling up from the Earth's and the universe's own bountiful potential. [As we have seen], it is more [reasonable and] appropriate to conceive of God as the ultimate depth and ground of nature's resourcefulness than as a magical intruder.*[1]

This physical foundation of carbon compounds manifests the evolving capacity of love continuing to spill over into ever new disclosures of divine love. This leads us to the heart of the relationship between God and evolution: God, as evolving limitless love, continues evolving through her/his beloved Cosmos with ever new and more impassioned ecstatic expression.

The fact that many in religion have tried to raise defensive arguments against evolution has proven severely obstructive to them, to religion, and, most importantly, to the march of evolution itself. God must reside within the evolving process as its fundament just as in all material expressions. We have seen that God and evolution walk "hand in hand down the aisle" sharing a physically and spiritually embracing explanation of God, Cosmos and ourselves.

Delio quotes N. Berdyaev: "Evolution reflects dynamic life, as matter evolves to spirit. The emergent Christ in evolution is not only the process of divine created unfolding life, but the evolution of God as well."[2]

We can trace evolution as follows: the Trinitarian Spirit of God present throughout the **Big Bang** initiating evolution into the **non-**

---

[1] Haught, *Responses To 101 Questions on God and Evolution* (NY: Paulist Presss, 2001), 23.
[2] Delio, *The Emergent Christ*, 3.

living which evolves toward the **living** which evolves toward **consciousness**, which evolves toward **Christ**, de Chardin's **Omega Point**. This evolutionary process proceeds with God as its abiding origin, foundation, energy, and goal. This is why understanding Christ (the fullness and exemplar of God, truth and goodness in each of us) as modeled by Jesus of Nazareth is elemental and vital in our search for wholeness which constitutes holiness.

This process of searching, which is the driver of evolution, rises from the dynamism of love [amorization, Chapter 6] which by nature is energized by the desire for improvement. The whole Cosmos, with God as fundament and humanity as reflective, forms one whole reality, but the whole is not static. It is becoming; it is evolving toward love's fullness, the Omega Point of reality, the fullness of truth and love, the Risen Christ.

As an example, every living part, when injured or ill, seeks, through many distinctive processes, to recover wholeness as in the healing of an abrasion. The present holon of creation as a whole is ever searching for the next more complex whole. Each part of the whole also continues to search for greater wholeness.

We, as searching parts and wholes, call this "the journey of life" not only for self but also for the whole. This amorous relationship of the Spirit of God that bonds us in one whole, challenges us thereby to cherish all our sisters and brothers, indeed, the whole Cosmos. All is sacred because God pervades all; we live in a sacred sanctuary. Every relationship calls us to mutual love. The tree loves us by protecting, shading, and beautifying. We love this heavenly canopy not by recklessly chopping and sawing but by nourishing and enjoying it with our universal family members.

Once, while walking with a friend in a gorgeous garden, he stopped to kiss a "rosery" petal of red. I trembled within, realizing the enormous divine body of rich relationships awaiting in our lovely whole.

Incarnation is the greatest! Each new moment of experience signals the unceasing incarnation of Christ, not the historical Jesus, but the cosmic Christ, the Christ of evolution to whom each of us helps to give birth. We remember however the counsel of Selesius: "Christ could be born a thousand times in Bethlehem – but all in vain, until he is born in me."[3] Because the divine Christ is called to fruition in each of us, we are bound together by the Spirit of Christ in all of us.

We can now realize more deeply that all created beings intersect and interact with each other and God. We are wholes, but also parts of one all-encompassing wondrous whole in Christ. This recommends to all of us an ultra-familial relationship of love and compassion for each other. You are my treasure, and I am yours. Although we might choose to alter our expression of love pursuant to circumstance, person, or event, no experience can lessen our love for each other one iota. Multiply this by our countless relationships,

---

[3] Angelus Silesius, *The Cherubic Wanderer,* Translated by Maria Shrady (Mahwah, NJ: Paulist Press 1986).

and we begin to understand the world of divine surpassing loveliness in which we are privileged to participate. Consider that the love of a caring biological family symbolizes the loving fullness of our universal family.

How dare we violate another Christ who is a genuine sister or brother! Recall the words of Thomas Merton spoken two hours before his death: "The whole idea of compassion is based on a keen awareness of the interdependence of all these living and non-living things which are part of one another and all involved in one another."[4]

This acknowledgement forms for us the beginning of new daily life of engaging love, and compels three dramatic changes in our worldviews:

First, there is our attitude toward our environment.

Water, air, space, etc. All these proclaim God's pervasive embodiment in his/her own unique way. For example, when in high school, I found summer work at the prodigious sea-front Hotel Belmont on Cape Cod, Massachusetts. In this youngster's eyes, this 200 room, green and white palace was a city unto itself with its own service station, laundry, doctors' offices, cleaners, etc.: a picture of indestructibility.

Years later, I returned to see my old beloved bastion of stability. As I approached on Old Belmont Road, I was rudely shocked, for the rock-solid buildings were gone; the putting green, now weeds; the massive lobby and buildings absent; my spirit sank. There had been a fire; all I could now see from my solemn silence was sun, surf, and sand. Profoundly moved, I realized to my core the frailty of myself

---

[4]Thomas Merton, *Asia Journal of Thomas Merton* (NY: New Directions 1973), 341.

and my perceived idols. Indeed, I mused: even sun, surf, and sand are as mortal and transforming as I, and I have caring obligations even toward them. All of us are destined in some way for the beyond.

Also, what of our non-human living companions?

How well I remember Harley, my son's tiny male Yorky terrier, who delighted in romping through our backyard, giving and receiving the joy of living. One day, while walking with him in the yard, I had turned my attention to another interest when suddenly I heard this poignant whimper behind. Turning, I was horrified to see his tiny body in the powerful jaws of a pit-bull that had crawled beneath the fence separating our home and our neighbor's. I screamed: the pit bull dropped Harley and ran off. Harley was in shock. He would never again run and rejoice as freely in his grassy playground. Harley, the pit-bull, and I related to each other in that moment in dramatic fashion with lasting consequences for all.

Years later, upon his death, we buried Harley beneath his beloved green where, to this day, he still interacts as part of our saving whole. All of us are called to relate to each other including even our world's pit bulls because love, God, pervades all of us and all our experiences.

Then, there is our relationship with our reasoning brothers and sisters worldwide and, possibly, cosmically.

The front page of today's Florida Sun-Sentinel headlines a portion of our current culture. "Marauding Florida members inspire violence." Most of us are not marauding in that sense, but we do often seek our own interests even at the expense of others. Unfortunately, I, with many others in Florida, share a history of investing in real estate always with the goal of unrestrained profit. I remember repeating within myself in those days the same question: "How can I maximize return on my money?" The truly Christian question would be "What is fair profit; what is just"? Christianity can be so demanding!

Whatever one's religion might be, or even if absent, serving and manifesting the cosmic Christ in our brothers and sisters presents the greatest challenge of all. It demands a traumatic transformation of our very nature – a life-long courageous journey from self to Christly self. The demands of this journey exceed the simple golden rule of *"Love your neighbor as yourself"*, Lev. 19:18. Christianity requires us to love as Jesus loved unto: death: "This is my commandment: Love one another, as I have loved you." (John 15:12)

As we seek Christ, we remember that he resides in all daily events and persons of our lives. Accordingly, we revere Christ in all these. That is the ultimate reason why we treasure our daily living and relationships. Thus, our joys and pains, all our Earthy relationships, comprise God's inner terrestrial chambers wherein we exult, and utter our gratitude for being there. Herein, lays the grandeur, the divine value of the material world and its events. Herein, we discover our daily resurrection, our salvation.

I wrote in a previous book that we think of resurrection as one event occurring to Jesus after his death. That is true, but resurrection also represents one more continuous gushing of God's outflowing love. Humanity's bizarre attempt to kill, slayed Jesus on that fated day, but also unwittingly provided the opportunity for God to unleash his Christ of love with powerful impact on us today.[5]

Our resurrection points to rising through our daily trials and pains to respond with love in all circumstances with our Earthen and

---

[5] Norman Carroll, *Miracles, Messages, and Metaphors: A Key to Understanding the Bible* (Austin, TX: Synergy Books, 2010),304.

cosmic sisters and brothers. This bespeaks the spiritual birth, the incarnation of Christ in each of us. Truly, Christ comes to his people through the ages to the degree they accept Jesus' life of compassion, courage, and sensitivity. Therefore, we observe that creation, incarnation, and resurrection (indeed, all events in our lives) form the chapters of that book of reality entitled *God Is Coming to All, So All Might Come to Him.*

Resurrection bridges the historical Jesus and the Risen Christ. To clarify, during his Earthly life, Jesus loved fully, and so, after proving this fullness of love in his life and especially through his death, he rose fully because God who is love accepts love fully. We, as part of God's creation, share in this victory over death insofar as we love. Likewise, insofar as we reject love here, to that degree, we choose not to participate in love hereafter. And that sounds like hell to me.

Whenever there is change (and there is always change), something known is abandoned, and something unknown is approached. Thus, change introduces uncertainty, danger, and often self-doubt. The outstanding example of such change is death. Death, O'Murchu writes, is both a natural and supernatural dimension of life "recycling its [life's] resources not into a mindless merry-go-round that never goes anywhere, but a process resembling a spiral always moving to realms of greater depth as evolution begets new possibilities for the death and transformation of old forms."[6]

Death and evolution are thus diametrically opposed. Death bespeaks cessation of life and movement while evolution presumes continuing life and becoming. Cosmic and Earthly life, evidenced by informed science and sound theology, testify to the supremacy of evolution and the death of death. Our Earthen life and death serve

---

[6] O'Murchu, op cit., *Evolutionary Faith,* 201.

as the ante-room to the divine-living room in the same home of life called love where we live before and after death.

Reverend Brenning Manning tells the following true story that illustrates this transcendent love. Richard Selzer, MD performed surgery to remove a tumor from a young lady's left cheek but was forced to sever her left facial nerve in the process. It left her mouth in a grotesque, palsy-like grimace. Later, he accompanied her husband to her bedside.

Upon seeing her distorted face in a hand mirror, she dissolved in anguished tears, and asked her husband: "Will it be permanent?" "Yes", her husband whispered from his own heartbreak; "the doctor had to sever the nerve." He paused, then bent over her, winked at her, and remarked, "You know: I find, it's rather cute." As he bent to kiss her, he twisted his lips to match hers whispering, "Now, we have a new bond between us", and her eyes glistened with hope. Dr. Selzer stepped back, numbed in silence as he realized he was in the presence of a hero of humanity, a true lover who was raising his beloved from a troubled tomb.

Those who deny life after death are forced to admit that all created beings of Earth and the entire Cosmos are loved into existence, and guided in continuing evolution throughout their existence for 13.7 billion years and counting. Then, they state, suddenly all this constant evolutional order and progressing cease, pursuant to death. Suddenly, an unwanted and untoward stillness and nothingness descend without justification, precedent, or explanation. The whole course of evolutional inheritance and progression ends in one moment. Who can believe this? Hardly possible! There is no extinction; there is only transformation!

To fear death becomes absurd; to fight death, counterproductive. "Death is swallowed up in victory." Death, where is your victory?

Death, where is your sting? (1 Cor.15:54) "Rather, we need to see our personal deaths as a transformative reconnection with the great energy fields of God's beloved creation", writes O'Murchu.[7] Death represents our greatest and final opportunity to evolve into our full capacity on Earth, into the cosmic Christ, the Risen One, Love itself.

Death introduces all creation into more intimate divine life signaled by victory through and over death and its minions of daily pain. Where there's life, there's resurrection; where there's resurrection, there's Christ; and where there's Christ, there are we, his beloved.

Despite their moments of triumph over daily mini-deaths and pains, many can't see physical signs of life beyond death, and accordingly, reject resurrection. By accepting and living the truth that we are holonic sisters and brothers with God in the ultimate whole of evolving love, we ensure our transforming into love. If God, who is love, exists before, during, and after all temporalities, then, so does life in some form. Transcendent love and life can't be limited by mere created time and space.

The truth is, all of us, do experience signs of life overcoming death throughout our entire cosmic whole. See the death of tulips in May, only to rise again as tulips in full bloom next April. What of the death of celestial stars even as others are born?

I remember well the day my grandfather died as another grandchild broke through into life. Some might object, "These are different individuals; the same individual does not rise." Such a person is thinking solely of the physical and individual entity. All of us belong to the ultimate whole whose parts are constantly changing not suddenly ceasing. Again, science and religion wed, for physicists tell us matter never ceases; it changes as water into steam or wood to ash. Resurrection and science are wed in love and truth.

---

[7] O'Murchu, op cit., *Adult Faith*, 193.

Many of us have a blind spot. We think of death without its counterpart, resurrection, as though death were greater than life, love, and God; as if death had final authority in the Cosmos. If one strips death of resurrection, then there **is** reason to fear the unknown oblivion of death. But one can't hold one side of a coin without holding the other: death and resurrection can't be separated for humans when all of creation proclaims their oneness. This represents the Paschal Mystery, the central teaching of Jesus. Evolution defeats finality; love defeats death.

The resurrection of Jesus is not his private affair, but the paradigm for all humans. Paul refers to the "*spiritual body*" after death, 1 Cor. 15:44. He means the whole person shot through with God's Spirit of love enduring fully through death. Paul certainly includes the entire Body of the cosmic Christ. By accepting God's Spirit fully, Jesus, the whole person and part of our ultimate whole, rose fully, and so we shall rise like him unto life to the degree we live his life of love. Phillip Larkin "cuts to the chase" with this line in his poem An Arundel's Tomb, "What will survive of us is love."

Behold! Our life becomes a journey of the sacred ultimate whole from moment to moment of ever-deeper engagement with love. This Spirit forms the grounding of our origin, presence, death, resurrection, and destiny, all in one human-divine experience. God's Spirit of love appears fully in just one person, Jesus of Nazareth, but does appear to varying degree in the rest of us.

Cardinal Joseph Ratzinger (later Pope Benedict XVI) writes in Dominus Jesus: "The Lord is the goal of human history: the focal point of the desires of history and civilization, the center of mankind, the joy of all hearts, and the fulfillment of all aspirations."[8]

---

[8]Joseph Cardinal Ratzinger, Prefect of Congregation of the Doctrine of the Faith: "Dominus Jesus" (Vatican City, Vatican Press 2000) para.15.

Not surprising that we are called to be a people of trust and joy in the supremacy of love which de Chardin calls "the infallible sign of the presence of God"

PRAYER

Lord Jesus, you trusted in your Father's love through death, and you were rewarded by overcoming death and rising beyond time and space, into life eternal. Grant us the insight and ability to express your courage, trust, and compassion knowing that we will experience with you truly risen life. What a privilege to share life with you, and to experience love with you now and forever! Amen! Alleluia!

SUMMARY

All of us have experienced bodily abrasions of various kinds, and they heal. But you have considered why? Could this be one more case of searching for wholeness? This search extends through all reality and demonstrates one more example of the continuing incarnation of God. Incarnation represents God's ongoing universal adaptive birth in creation. This view of divinity compels three changes in our worldview: toward the non-living, the living, and toward our brothers and sisters, for all is holy and merits our reverence.

Religions' role is to promote this world of worship. Divine love powers such divinely transcendent birthing and lends credence to resurrection. For how could supreme love suddenly and totally abandon all beloved creation? Otherwise, we would have to admit that death reigns over life and love. Logical order negates such possibility. Yes, we are destined to live and love beyond time and space.

GROUP DISCUSSION QUESTIONS

1. Explain the fallacy of this statement: Death is final, and love dies with it.

2. If all, including God, IS evolving, then death is also evolving. Into what?

3. How could the familial love we experience before death symbolize the quality of our universal love after death?

4. How do you justify treasuring our environment?

5. How can we view death as opportunity?

6. We have focused on all reality representing the flowing of divine love. How can life, death, and resurrection fit that scenario?

7. Could the acceptance of God's pervasive love introduce heaven? If so, would not its denial introduce hell? Where then do heaven and hell exist?

10

THAT ALL MAY BE ONE

*"All are but parts of one stupendous whole
whose body nature is and God, the soul."*

Alexander Pope

Karen Armstrong exclaims, "When we use the word 'holy' today, we usually refer to a state of moral excellence. The Hebrew *Kaddosh* [meaning holy], however, has nothing to do with morality as such, but means 'otherness', a radical separation. The apparition of Yahweh on Mt. Sinai [in the Burning Bush] had emphasized the immense gulf that had suddenly yawned between man and the divine world. Now the Seraphs were crying: 'Yahweh is other! Other! Other!'"[1] Indeed, the Hebrews would not even pronounce God's name, and believed that anyone who saw God would surely die. This mighty chasm between God and humanity was reflected in the Hasidim "the separated ones" who gave rise most likely to the Pharisees and the Essenes. The Jewish people viewed them also as separated and therefore holy.

---

[1]Karen Armstrong, *A History of God* (NY: Ballantine Books 1994), 41.

Identifying the holy with separation continues in much Christian thinking through the centuries. The early Christians witnessed a fleeing of holy ones into the deserts as solitaries. Later, monks, such as cloistered Benedictines, Carmelites, and Carthusians, among others, sought separation. Today's rule of mandated celibacy among all clerics and religious in the Roman Catholic Church serves to continue this same notion. These examples are laudable, but still prove the point that separation and holiness walk hand-in-hand in our Judaic-Christian tradition.

The power of separation certainly breeds mystery which has its necessary place. However, such separation has tragically led much of the Church of Christ into a hierarchical clerical system of ordained who view themselves not only as separate but sadly, also as superior. I remember being taught years ago in a Roman Catholic seminary that togetherness was nice but second in adherence to Catholic doctrine and hierarchical authority. Sadly, we have rarely reflected on how Jesus would have immediately rejected that thinking.

This interdependence, of separation and holiness, flows "in the blood" of the Christian psyche even today. Could this be one reason Christian authorities and the baptized neither understood nor accepted Teilhard's work of creating wholes, and union which these pages discuss. This refusal has repressed human togetherness and its fruits of love, peace, and unity.

Talk about separation! Some estimate over twenty-two thousand Christian denominations stand alive and well. Many call this scandalous.

Rev. Paul Watson, the founder of the Graymoor Friars (Franciscan Friars of the Atonement), the only religious community to be received as a body into Roman Catholicism, was so disturbed with multiple belief systems that in the early twentieth century he founded the Chair of Unity Octave. This was a period of eight days of prayer (January 18 – 25) for Christian unity, meaning the return of separated brethren to the Roman Catholic Church, and the octave was liturgically assigned those dates.

Being a member of the Graymoor Friars at that time, I recall praying in community each night of the octave for the conversion of Lutherans, Anglicans, Jews, and many others, even lapsed Catholics, to full communion with Rome. This return to Rome represented the ideal of Christian ecumenism for me and nearly all Catholics at that time. The motto for the Graymoor community was *"That they all may be one"* John 17:21

Jesus did pray these words, but he was certainly not referring to the unity of these denominations. Indeed, Christianity itself did not even exist during his physical presence on Earth. He was praying that all God's created would enter into more intimate union with God in each other, patterned on his own oneness with God and creation. Surely, Jesus had no knowledge of the scientific explanation of the Cosmos, but his understanding and his love of God secured for him oneness with his Father whom he found in all he touched.

We discover God through material creation because of God's gapless union with it, thus making the material world most worthy of our participation, reverence, and love. We acknowledge the whole evolving creation (including the unimaginable Cosmos), as one incredible energy manifesting God's love from within.

Joseph Campbell tells the following story: "Of the deeply troubled woman who came to the Indian saint and sage Ramakrishna, saying, 'Oh master, I do not find that I love God.' And [Ramakrishna] asked, 'Is there nothing, then, that you love?' 'To this she answered, 'My little nephew' and he said to her, 'There is your love and service to God, in your love and service to that child.'"[2]

Teilhard de Chardin concludes that because all of us seek truth and love in each other, we are one. You and I exist, and re-create each other. Truly, we are already united with God and each other. In a real sense, you and I are one.

We have seen that a primary insight of Teilhard lies in God's love pervading through all, for nothing can exist separate from God. Thus, we can rejoice in one supreme love: God embracing all of us fully in astounding unity from within. Those who seek solitude or celibate ordination merit our admiration, but their vocation calls primarily for their being of greater loving service to our whole according to their charism, but not part of an autocratic clericalism.

Because of this loving union with all of us, God calls us directly to his heart as well as through the mediation of all we experience. We can now appreciate more clearly the precedence of union with God over membership in any particular church. However, church does have sublime value insofar as it leads us to such union.

Thomas Berry declares, "the four basic human establishments:" the political, economic, educational, and religious communities ... give basic rights and values [only] to the human ... At present, there is a devastating gap between the human community and the [rest of the

---

[2] Joseph Campbell, *The Hero's Journey* (Novato, CA: New World Library, 1990), 40.

Earthen] community."³ The cosmic community is scarcely considered at all.

Togetherness! Compassion! Peace! These are the cries rising from our battered mother Earth, disenfranchised humans, the Cosmos, and our ignored God within all of it. Pope Francis asserts: "This sister [mother Earth] now cries out to us because of the harm we have inflicted on her by our irresponsible use and abuse of the goods with which God has endowed her. We have come to see ourselves as her lord and master, entitled to plunder her at will.⁴ Berry agrees, "Now there is a need to adopt a new sense of a self-emergent universe as a sacred mode whereby the divine becomes present."⁵

This divine indwelling in all created beings forms the foundation for universal unity. However, the whole United Nations fails to view the boundless wholeness of the universe (by excluding the inanimate) declaring, "Mankind is a part of nature.... [and] every form of life is unique, warranting respect regardless of its [usefulness] to man."⁶ God would discern our unity far differently than we, for most of us see oneness with others deriving from family, nation, church, or even humanity. God, however, manifests ever deeper union with all material creation from ages past even to the Big Bang and to all future possibilities.

This is the ultimate whole of reality to which we referred in Chapter 1. God and all the created remain forever in union. We erect walls of division such as gays-straight, rich-poor, black-white, East-West, Catholic-Protestant, and many others. God seeks to have us tear

---

³Thomas Berry, *The Christian Future and the Fate of Earth* (Maryknoll, NY, Orbis Books, 2009), 112.

⁴ Pope Francis, "Laudio Si" (Vatican Press, May 24, 2015) para. 2

⁵ Berry, op cit., 115.

⁶ "The Charter for Nature": UN General Assembly, 1982.

down from within our hearts, these walls, and, with him, co-create a new universal world of compassion and peace.

Individualism, control, and violence seem to belie these pages that breathe of love and unity. For we humans, as one part of the whole Earth, are threatening to destroy the whole thus destroying us as well. Such madness in the names of illusory power and profit! We need desperately reconciliation, with all our sisters and brothers, with Earth, and a Cosmos already being militarized. Time is of the essence, for the Arctic is melting, the water contaminant, the air fetid and military reigns as king. Ninety eight percent of scientists agree that humanity bears responsibility for an impending ecological cataclysm.

Fraile writes: "Reconciliation is a creative power of life and love; it is the prelude of total oneness."[7] The unity we discuss herein is not a mere coming together of peoples but a reconciliation of all created beings by loving and caring for each other appropriately despite our cultural and constitutive differences. This certainly includes our so-called enemies whether global or personal.

True religion is foundational and essential to human reconciliation and its consequential unity of the whole (God, Cosmos, and humanity) because only religion can summon our whole beings to reconciliation and love. We see business contracts, vows of marriage and international agreements routinely broken because they often represent specious bargains of convenience or usefulness. Religion, however, reaches from the heart, and demands commitment from our core.

Additionally, religion calls us to embrace all our brothers and sisters, not just friends. Finally, religion (meaning a bonding) by its very nature, calls us together with enduring dedication to excelling

---

[7] Peter Fraile, *God Within Us* (Cha: Loyola University Press, 1986), 62.

motives and goals beyond our self-interest. One could say, "Healthy religion remains our only hope." Delio writes,

> *The convergence of religions must be centered on love, with each religion expressing love and union with the divine [and all brothers and sisters] in its own particular way ... The greatest danger of religion is to assume [for itself superiority or] any type of sovereign power because love always lives for the other ... Religion degenerates into religiosity when God is absolutized by constructing foundations that are purported to be immutable.*[8]

Current examples would include any church claiming infallibility as if it were divine, or a mosque or temple claiming exclusive access to the prophet or asserting itself as the only (chosen) people. Any belief system insisting on its own absolute truth is implicitly claiming, "We are right, and all who don't agree are wrong. Further, we have truth already and therefore need not search for further truth." Such arrogance destroys inquiry, a basic reason for human existence. Such religion closes itself to further truth and as cultural knowledge grows, that religion becomes decidedly more fallible, bereft, and finally irrelevant. Any system proclaiming its infallibility proves its fallibility.

Rather than making outrageous claims of tribal superiority, let us pool resources and insights so that together the great religions can offer the universal fundamental values of meditation, compassion, nonviolence, justice, and peace. These are common and fundamental to all genuine religions.

---

[8] Delio, *The Unbearable Wholeness of Being*, 112, 113.

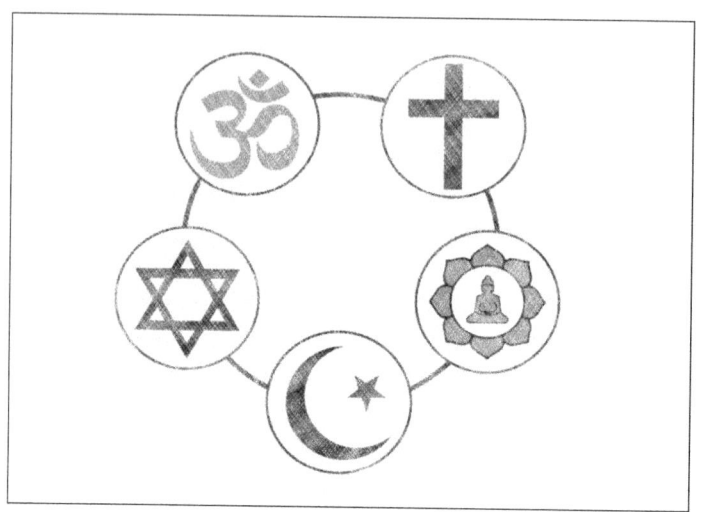

I recall a young Christian woman counselling with me, for she wished to become Muslim. Her family objected bitterly, and she came to me in tears. Her parents threatened "to throw her out of the house." What to advise? Finally, I explained to her that she ought to join that community that maximized her touching the God of love present within her and all creation. She decided eventually to remain a Christian but as a reformer.

These aforementioned values (meditation, compassion, nonviolence, justice, and peace) reflective of the divine, raise people of all persuasions to the heights. William Johnston comments: "Through co-operation in [this] great venture, sincere believers [and none] of all religions can form friendship and community, they can travel the path of union."[9]

Every sincere religious quest for unity needs human organization. After careful reflection, I have arrived at a possible starting point. I surely, do not claim it as the final word, but hopefully it will initiate

---

[9]William Johnston, *The Inner Eye of Love: Mysticism and Religion* (London: Collins, 1978), 78.

discussion. According to this plan, each religious body would retain its own governance and foundation document; for example, Islam and the Koran, but members of each religion would recognize and affirm the need and foundation of the aforementioned values. Further, they would accept, and promote their role as part of a greater whole totally committed to these values.

If these values are to endure with lasting impact, organization must enshrine them. Your author was privileged to speak at the 2015 Parliament of World Religions in Salt Lake City, Utah, which attracted over 10,000 people. Formerly, the Parliament convened every five years, but now demand for greater frequency necessitates bi-annual conferences. It brings together representatives of all significant religions with renowned speakers such as the Dalai Lama. Surely, the Parliament would constitute an ideal vehicle to promote worldwide religious reconciliation in order to progress this movement of fundamental religious values.

The Charter for Compassion, initiated by Karen Armstrong in 2009, would provide a framework for a compelling foundation document of the entire Parliament. We quote from the Charter: "The principle of compassion lies at the heart of all worthy religious, ethical, and spiritual traditions, calling us always to treat all others as we wish to be treated ourselves." The parliament and charter would not set religions or denominations in competition with each other; nor form another religion. Rather, they construct a foundation for **all** religions and a framework with which any genuine religion could agree, for these values remain precious to all humanity.

The "theology of wholeness" we have espoused, proclaims desperately a clarion call for such a substratum of support for all worthy religions, and would not threaten their solidarity. Inter-religious competitions, conservative-progressive intra-religious antagonism, violence, and neglect: the hostility of these and all religious factions would be revealed as counterproductive and ultimately inhumane. A refusal to participate by any major religious body would clearly expose its obstructionist posture to these unquestioned human values, and weaken it at its own peril.

Despite its universal appeal, such a vision might appear unthinkable because of some religionists who consider denominational affinities more compelling than their evolutionary obligation of promoting greater wholes and ultimate unity. "Whole-making" is the actual root meaning of the word catholic, and someday, which I will not see, this essential quality will assuredly manifest itself throughout our religious spectrum. To realize greater wholes, each religious body must become willing to accept its own human limitations so that all can contribute in a universal quest for truth and love. Delio writes, "As long as religions remain in conflict, evolution is thwarted in its forward direction and the Earth suffers the pains of division."[10]

Religion's chief task remains to bond together the parts and wholes of all reality; that is, to midwife the continuing universal incarnation, and the living maturation of those aforementioned community values portrayed herein. The evolutionary findings of science provide the ideal canvas upon which religion can paint its masterpiece of divine, cosmic, and human lovemaking. Such is the hallmark of enlightened religious search. Paul describes it as such: *"We are well aware that the whole creation, until this time, has been groaning in labor pains."* (Romans 8:22)

Because the incarnation is truly God emerging everywhere, every created being, at every moment, becomes uniquely incarnational. This is the incarnational unity of which Merton spoke just weeks before his death. "My dear brothers and sisters, we are already one,

---

[10]Delio, op cit., *The Unbearable Wholeness*, 108.

but we imagine that we are not. What we have to be [Christ], is what we are."[11] Truly, we are one now, but seek greater oneness.

All of us are continuing our vital search for truth and love. In this sense, we share the same goal of which many remain unaware. This search bonds us as other Christs so that we are united in origin, foundation, goal, and destiny. Still, how often we commit violence toward each other, and do so even in the name of our God of peace.

We observed in Chapter 7 that God is calling us to be Christs (saviors), but for Christians that Christliness must follow the example of Jesus. Jesus lived for this visionary reason: to provide us with God's idea (a blueprint) of what being Christ means. To prove our need for a model Christ, we recall that some people looked on Hitler as a christ, a savior of the nation, but his leadership did not conform with the ideals of Jesus, and that was in his case disingenuous to the extreme.

As a Christ, Jesus understood that God lives in union with his whole beloved creation, and Jesus thirsted for that union to become ever more expressive in all God's children even like unto his union. The emerging of this Christ living in our lives includes our attitudes toward death and resurrection. Delio suggests,

> *The resurrection shows us the personal love of God [for humanity] in the person of Jesus ... What resurrection says is that human life has cosmic meaning in the heart of love ... we die individually, but we are part of a greater whole. Christ belongs to the whole ... Christ represents the capacity of every person to live in love and hence in God.*[12]

---

[11]National Catholic Reporter, "Thomas Merton at 100", Dec. 5-18, 2014, 1a.

[12]Delio, *The Unbearable Wholeness of Being*, 105.

By rising, Jesus defeats death and, because he is human our fears of death. Therefore, we live and die secure and safe in his and our ever-growing victorious mutual love-union. Thus death, the greatest agent of fear and division ever known, is overcome by resurrection, the greatest agent of love and union ever revealed.

Death and resurrection become the most promising, momentous, and transcendent event of our Earthen lives. Paul refers to the magnificence of God's designs by writing, *"What no eye has seen, and no ear has heard, what the mind of man cannot visualize; all that God has prepared for those who love him."* (1 Corinthians 2:9)

We have traditionally understood this passage as promising an objective gift of heaven from a benevolent God who would welcome us to his throne room of divinity and goodness on high. Rather, we now reflect on a universe (of which we are now a part) evolving with convergence toward that one Omega Point, the Risen Christ, the home of love and oneness. This is heaven. Thus, the unity of all created beings is not fractured or disturbed by death or by any lesser challenge.

In what does this unity consist? Paul tells us no one fully knows except the Spirit of God. We can, however, competently search, for God's Spirit resides in us. One thing is certain: unity does not demand uniformity. Unity does not mandate that all of us accept the same precise teachings, or live the same lifestyle, but God as love does consistently call us from our depths to live in profound meditation, compassion, nonviolence, justice, and peace.

We reflect on the boundless Cosmos still hurtling outward in its evolving complexity; the fantastic array of non-living and living creatures both terrestrial and possibly beyond; and the possible myriad forms of consciousness known and unknown. All of this is sustained and energized by God's pervasive indwelling Spirit toward that point of ultimate unity, the Omega Point.

Teilhard's Omega Point ought not to be viewed as a finishing line in a race. Rather, it encompasses all created beings of every space and time throughout the universe, surging ever onward toward their full evolving capacity of love which is the Omega Point, the Risen Christ who is also evolving. This explains the convergence of which Teilhard speaks. We may liken this Omega Point to a lighthouse the beams of which attract those endangered, to the safety of homeport away from the rocks of destruction. Jesus, that beam with the brightest capacity, (created beings form assisting beams) plays the lead role in teaching and inspiring the faithful in this rapidly changing axial culture. Keep your eye fixed on this lighthouse!

Some might consider this explanation of reality as too optimistic even "polyanish." However, it clarifies the roles of God and all created beings in a very reasonable way while also integrating scientific findings. Love is the supreme human activity, and plays that role in an appropriate and central manner. All this results in an insightful exegesis of what is transpiring in our marvelous, mysterious reality: Christ (the powerful evolving of divine love in all creation) is divinizing all creation. As a result, we treasure appropriately this whole material world of matter, and sing with Teilhard de Chardin,

> *Blessed be you, mighty matter, irresistible march of evolution, reality ever newborn ... [who] force us to go ever further and further in our pursuit of the truth. Blessed be you ... who... by overflowing and dissolving our narrow standards or measurements reveal to us the dimensions of God.*[13]

---

[13]Teilhard de Chardin, *Him of the Universe* (NY: Harper and Row, 1965), 69.

So, instead of condemning or fleeing the material world, we discover our God of love therein. This is the real union to which we of the world both cling and aspire.

Some accused Teilhard of espousing a pantheistic order according to which all created beings are identified with God. I suggest such critics do not sufficiently appreciate the surpassing strands of unifying inviolate love which God and we effect. This is not pantheistic, but does illustrate the physical and spiritual intimacy of God and God's created "images." Enlightened Christianity is not Pantheism because unity is not identity.

Pantheism destroys the beloved and the union with it, for where there is only one; there is no togetherness, no union. Our union with God rests not on identity but on the union of two or more in every wonder of love. Thus, Teilhard exclaims: "I can be saved only by becoming one with the universe," for that is where God is found.[14]

Years ago, Eugene Boylan entitled his biography of Christ, *The Tremendous Lover.* That title applies to Jesus and each of us because Christ lives in us. As a Christ, you are a tremendous lover. Certainly, loving has different applications, but each of God's beloved creatures merits our appropriate love. I owe you my love, as noted in Chapter 4, because you and God are one, and you owe me the same. These bonds weave the munificent fibers that maintain the universal web of unity in which we all participate with God.

Therefore, there is no better way to conclude our quest than for me to tell you with all sincerity, "I love you", not because of your religion, nationality, wealth, nor even because of your persevering through these pages. I love you because of who you are: my sister

---

[14]Teilhard de Chardin, *Christianity and Evolution*, 128.

or brother in the becoming oneness of our whole, forever bonded by our loving God in all.

As for Jesus, he is calling us to spend our daily lives in search of our Omega Point, that evolving fulfillment of the whole self with indestructible incarnational love for all creation. This: the greatest challenge to which humanity has ever been summoned. This evolutional growth of Christ in you and me magnifies the 13.7 billion year surge of divine love throughout this blessed Cosmos. It also represents the true second coming of Christ.

We as the "People of God" have, as previously noted, never realized this second appearance of Christ occurring now, through us and in us. God is inviting us to participate in the mystery of divine impassioned love engulfing all creation and making us one.

Thus, we resolve here and now to begin each day with at least a ten-minute commitment to perform in Christ a specific act of love for a particular person, object, or experience we shall encounter today. May this form a powerful habit from this moment now and beyond. This: our evolving response to that prayer of Jesus, our personal and communal lover, "That they all may be one! (John 17:21)

PRAYER

Lord God, you reside in and energize all your children (cosmic, Earthen, and human). Your love in all of us makes us one with you and each other. We promise to live our daily lives in love with all creation as we journey to you through each other. In this way, we fulfill your prayer that they all may be one by giving birth to your son again, and again in our small corner of the Cosmos until that day when you draw us and all your beloved to your heart of pure, ecstatic embrace. Amen. Alleluia!

SUMMARY

So distressing that holiness in our consciousness necessitates separation, for its opposite, wholeness, comprises the true mark of healthy holiness. We, created and uncreated, constitute one whole. Many still believe that Jesus, when praying that all may be one, prayed for denominational unity.

However, as a Jew, he was praying that all would seek oneness with God who is truth and love. Jesus recognized that unity could not result from mere human motivations (as altruistic they might be). Divine love (willingness to sacrifice one's life for the other) is needed. Our human unity must model on the love of the immanent Trinity.

Because we are societal, organization is necessary to proclaim, structure, and monitor our religions. Fortunately, all major religions rest with variables on the same universal values: meditation, compassion, nonviolence, justice, and peace. These spring from that divine love which surges through all created beings. Thus, we call on the Parliament of World Religions to act as an underlying agent to promote these divine and human values so fundamental to our religions.

Further, we can envision the Charter for Compassion serving in principle as the foundation document for the Parliament. We are well aware that substantial organizational planning is needed, but it is urgent we begin to align together religious forces so these values will assume a primary and fundamental position in human consciousness. What a grand incarnation this would be in answer to Christ's prayer, "That all may be one."

GROUP DISCUSSION QUESTIONS

1. What did Jesus mean when he prayed "That they all may be one?"
2. If all of us are already one, what bonds us together?
3. What walls would Jesus have us tear down?
4. What is your response to one who states, "We have many human enemies?"
5. Why is healthy religion needed so desperately at this time?
6. If we are already in union, why seek union?
7. Distinguish the Omega Point from a finish line.

OTHER BOOKS
FROM PACEM IN TERRIS PRESS

PADRE MIGUEL
A Memoir of My Catholic Missionary Experience in Bolivia
amidst Postcolonial Transformation of Church and State
Michael J. Gillgannon, 2018

POSTMODERN ECOLOGICAL SPIRITUALITY
Catholic-Christian Hope for the Dawn of a Postmodern Ecological Civilization Rising
from within the Spiritual Dark Night of Modern Industrial Civilization
Joe Holland, 2017

JOURNEYS TO RENEWED CONSECRATION
Religious Life after Fifty Years of Vatican II
Emeka Obiezu, OSA & John Szura, OSA, Editors, 2017

THE CRUEL ELEVENTH-CENTURY IMPOSITION OF
WESTERN CLERICAL CELIBACY
A Monastic-Inspired Attack on Catholic Episcopal & Clerical Families
Joe Holland, 2017

LIGHT, TRUTH, & NATURE
Practical Reflections on Vedic Wisdom & Heart-Centered Meditation
In Seeking a Spiritual Basis for Nature, Science, Evolution, & Ourselves
Thomas Pliske, 2017

THOMAS BERRY IN ITALY
Reflections on Spirituality & Sustainability
Elisabeth M. Ferrero, Editor, 2016

PETER MAURIN'S
ECOLOGICAL LAY NEW MONASTICISM
A Catholic Green Revolution Developing
Rural Ecovillages, Urban Houses of Hospitality,
& Eco-Universities for a New Civilization
Joe Holland, 2015

PROTECTION OF RELIGIOUS MINORITIES
A Symposium Organized by Pax Romana at the United Nations
and the United Nations Alliance of Civilizations
Dean Elizabeth F. Defeis & Peter F. O'Connor, Editors, 2015

BOTTOM ELEPHANTS
Catholic Sexual Ethics & Pastoral Practice in Africa:
The Challenge of Women Living within Patriarchy
& Threatened by HIV-Positive Husbands
Daniel Ude Asue, 2014

CATHOLIC LABOR PRIESTS
Five Giants in the United States Catholic Bishops Social Action Department
Volume I of US Labor Priests During the 20th Century
Patrick Sullivan, 2014

CATHOLIC SOCIAL TEACHING & UNIONS
IN CATHOLIC PRIMARY & SECONDARY SCHOOLS
The Clash between Theory & Practice within the United States
Walter "Bob" Baker, 2014

SPIRITUAL PATHS TO
A GLOBAL & ECOLOGICAL CIVILIZATION
Reading the Signs of the Times with Buddhists, Christians, & Muslims
John Raymaker & Gerald Grudzen, with Joe Holland, 2013

PACEM IN TERRIS
Its Continuing Relevance for the Twenty-First Century
(Papers from the 50th Anniversary Conference at the United Nations)
Josef Klee & Francis Dubois, Editors, 2013

PACEM IN TERRIS
Summary & Commentary for the Famous Encyclical Letter
of Pope John XXIII on World Peace
Joe Holland, 2012

100 YEARS OF CATHOLIC SOCIAL TEACHING
DEFENDING WORKERS & THEIR UNIONS
Summaries & Commentaries for Five Landmark Papal Encyclicals
Joe Holland, 2012

HUMANITY'S AFRICAN ROOTS
Remembering the Ancestors' Wisdom
Joe Holland, 2012

THE "POISONED SPRING" OF ECONOMIC LIBERTARIANISM
*Menger, Mises, Hayek, Rothbard: A Critique from
Catholic Social Teaching of the Austrian School of Economics*
Pax Romana / Cmica-usa
Angus Sibley, 2011

BEYOND THE DEATH PENALTY
The Development in Catholic Social Teaching
Florida Council of Catholic Scholarship
D. Michael McCarron & Joe Holland, Editors, 2007

THE NEW DIALOGUE OF CIVILIZATIONS
*A Contribution from Pax Romana
International Catholic Movement for Intellectual & Cultural Affairs*
Pax Romana / Cmica-usa
Roza Pati & Joe Holland, Editors, 2002

*This book and other books from Pacem in Terris Press,
are available at:*

www.amazon.com/books

www.ingramcontent.com/pod-product-compliance
Lightning Source LLC
Chambersburg PA
CBHW051059160426
43193CB00010B/1247